THE REALITY OF YOUR GREATNESS

A Personal Journey Through the Twelve Rays

Michael G. Love

SPARK Publications

Charlotte, North Carolina

The Reality of Your Greatness:
A Personal Journey Through the Twelve Rays
Michael G. Love

Copyright © 2018 by Michael G. Love. All rights reserved. No part of this book may be used or reproduced in any manner whatsoever without written permission from the author, except in the case of brief quotations embodied in critical articles or reviews. For permissions requests, please contact the author at roygreatness@gmail.com.

Designed, produced, and published by SPARK Publications, SPARKpublications.com
Charlotte, NC

Printed in the United States of America.
First Print Edition, March 2018, ISBN: 978-1-943070-34-3
E-book, March 2018, ISBN: 978-1-943070-35-0
Library of Congress Control Number: 2018935386

OCC019000   BODY, MIND & SPIRIT / Inspiration & Personal Growth
SEL031000   SELF-HELP / Personal Growth / General / Spirituality
REL062000   RELIGION / Spirituality

DEDICATION

I am dedicating this book to the person who made it all possible. When I say she is the reason for this book's very existence, I am not overstating her role in its production. I can not begin to express my gratitude for all the ways that she influenced the creation of this work.

Julie, I am forever grateful for all that you have done and the roles that you have played that have contributed to the realization of this book.

CONTENTS

PREFACE

This book is about us, humankind, being children of God. I believe we are at a point where we are, from a spiritual perspective, turning into teenagers. Each one of us has been through those teenage years. We can personally relate to the experience. Many of us have even raised teenagers ourselves. One of the things that teenagers want to change is their relationship with their parents. They don't want to be seen as children anymore.

They want to make their own decisions. They want to show their parents that they can be trusted. They want to set personal goals and then achieve them. They learn that some choices lead them closer to those goals and some lead them further away from their goals. This is how we learn discernment.

It is a time of great transformation for all of us here on this planet, in this dimension. I use the expression "this dimension" to reference our physical experience here on planet Earth. I believe many of us are searching for a new relationship with God (the Source, the Creator, All That Is, or whatever name you prefer to use). The Twelve Rays helped me do just that—create a new relationship with the entity I call All That Is.

My personal journey through the Twelve Rays began in the spring of 2005. That is when I began directly communicating with a small group of entities through a trance channel. I will refer to her as Julie throughout the book, although that is not her real name. Julie and I fondly refer to this group as "the Team." That experience changed my life forever. We have received information from them on a wide range of topics. One of the first topics they shared with us was the Twelve Rays.

There is, however, a much broader message that the Team communicated through all of the sessions. For me personally, working with the Rays was a way to embrace that broader message. I have distilled that message down to three words—you are more. The beauty of these three words is that no matter what or who you think yourself to be, you are still more. The human mind cannot contemplate the vastness of the more that you and I are beyond this dimension. And you could argue that it was never intended to be able to comprehend that greatness.

But the mind can understand that you are more than what you currently believe yourself to be. It is all well and good to read in this book or any book that you are more; it is quite another proposition to believe it and live it. I used the Twelve Rays to help me move from the knowing part to the visceral, emotional reality of being more.

There was an identifiable moment when that shift happened for me, and the Team gave me a hint that just one part was missing. A quick note of explanation here: the Team often refers to me as Simon. They use it to refer to a specific lifetime I experienced. Here is another bit of explanation that should help: throughout this book, the Team's comments will be in the font treatment you see below.

Here is what they told me nearly three years after I began working with them:

> *You too, Simon, are simply a thought, one thought away from everything, from all knowledge, from all mastery. The light is within you—just one thought away.*

During a channeling session about four years after the Team's comment above, I received an insight that seems to have been that one thought. I'm pretty sure it hasn't led yet to all knowledge, all mastery; I'm still working on that. But that one thought is that we are and have always been connected to our higher selves or, as I like to say, our whole selves. And our whole selves are connected to All That Is. When I embraced that concept, everything changed for me. I go into greater detail about that experience later in the book.

It is impossible for me to say that anyone reading this book is also one thought away from opening to a greater reality. What I can say with a high level of certainty is by understanding the Twelve Rays and using the tools provided in this book to help you work with the Rays, you can achieve the goals you planned for this lifetime, whatever they may be.

What This Book Is About

This book is about the children of God becoming teenagers and establishing a new relationship with God. There are many common experiences that can be included in any description of the teenage experience. What strikes me as the essence of the entire experience is this is the time when we become individuals. We examine all the information we have been given about the nature of things, how we should behave, what we should avoid, what we should believe in, and what we decide what makes sense to us personally. We keep what feels right, and we discard what doesn't.

We then set out on our life adventures looking for answers to the questions that remain. Many of us find there are new questions that we were totally unaware of. In other words, we didn't know what we didn't know. This can be overwhelming. Especially when life is happening all around us. Growing up and striking out on our own requires a significant amount of energy. It is easy to see how we can get distracted and no longer focus on searching for life's answers.

The funny thing is time passes quickly when you are distracted. My definition of a midlife crisis is when an individual realizes that he or she is not young anymore and still has all of these life questions outstanding. But I don't believe that humankind is having a midlife crisis. I believe that we are becoming teenagers. Some of us are questioning everything. Others are distracted and are just accepting things as they are and are likely headed in my opinion toward a midlife crisis at some time in the future.

How do we help those of us who are questioning everything? One way is to share our experiences. And that is what I have done here. I have shared with you my experience of finding out what I didn't know I didn't know. I had never heard of the Twelve Rays before, yet I found myself receiving instruction about them from beings in another dimension. They told me they are friends of mine, and they reminded me of other lifetimes here in this dimension that we shared together.

They told me that humankind was at a crossroads and that we could choose differently. We could choose grace and ease over pain and suffering. We could embrace our heritage as children of God and release the limiting beliefs we have about ourselves. They told me we could learn to create differently by focusing our attention on what we desired to manifest. And they told me we could bring more of our greatness into this dimension.

They told me that the Twelve Rays would help us to make all of this a reality. The journey that I share with you in this book begins with the First Ray and finishes with the Twelfth Ray. The information that I have about the Rays was given in a series of sessions with the Team. Needless to say, the journey still continues to this day.

The Twelve Rays are divided into three distinct groups. The first group of Rays is referred to as the Rays of Aspect. This group consists of the energy from the Source—or All That Is—that is our Divine Heritage. The second group, the Rays of Attributes, represents our human characteristics that enable us to have the unique experiences here in this dimension. The third group, the Rays of Soul Integration, consists of tools to help us to move forward in our evolution of Spirit here in this dimension. I go into all of this in greater detail in the following chapters.

When I decided it was time to write about the Twelve Rays, I created a seminar that I taught over several weeks in which I presented the material as it was received from the Team. I developed guided meditations for each class, which are included in this book and are available as recordings at TheTwelveRays.com.

An idea came to me over a year ago, and I have been developing it ever since. The Team has always presented the Rays as vibrating as a certain color, and that has been helpful for many individuals, myself included. I can imagine for example that the Second Ray is a luminescent aqua blue. But the Team also said they hear the Rays as notes. This got me thinking. Is it possible to create music that is blended with the energy of a certain Ray? How could I go about creating that and sharing it with others?

Then I remembered that my wonderfully gifted friend Richard Shulman has the ability to tune into an individual's energy and create a personal musical soul portrait using his keyboards. He has done it for me on a couple of occasions, and they are wonderful. As a matter of fact, I recall that the Team even commented on one of these pieces once. I wondered if Richard could focus in on the energy of a given Ray and play music that was blended with the energy of that particular Ray. We gave it a try, and it seems to work wonderfully.

Now I have a second way for everyone to relate to the energy of the Rays, and I am delighted to be able to share this with you. Please visit my website, TheTwelveRays.com/music, and you will be able to sample short clips of this music for free. You will also be able to keep current on where the music has taken us.

We are continuing to develop new insights in how to bring this energy of the Rays to life musically. Richard and I have created a compilation of musical tracks for each Ray. This compilation is available in CD format or as a downloadable MP3 file on the website realityofyourgreatness.com/music. For those of you who relate to music, I'm sure you will find this music very enjoyable. And hopefully it will help you connect to the energy of the Rays in a personal way.

How To Use This Book

Each of the Rays has its own chapter. The format of these Ray chapters is the same. I begin each one with the information that was provided to me by the Team. Then there is a short Stop and Feel section where I ask you to connect with the energy of the individual Ray. There is a short space that follows to write down your initial experience of the Ray. Feel free to either write in your book or use a separate notebook. The next section is a discussion. Imagine that you and I are sitting down one to one, and I am sharing with you some of my personal insights into that particular Ray. This section is followed by a meditation that is between fifteen and twenty minutes in duration. Each meditation has a longer section to write down your experiences. Again feel free to write this down wherever you are most comfortable. Keep in mind, it is important to write down your comments as soon as you finish the meditation. So have whatever you are using to write in handy before you start the meditation. Some chapters have more than one meditation. Each Ray chapter ends with a summary page. Here you will find the key concepts and learnings of the chapter.

Icons

The Ray chapters have the following icons.

 Stop and Feel icon—This is the section where I ask you to stop and feel the energy of Ray. This is a short exercise, and you should only spend a couple of minutes with it.

 Listen icon—This is an optional part of the stop and feel section. If you have the music that accompanies the book then play the music for the corresponding Ray here. This will be a little longer exercise with the music added. Check the length of each track to see how long the music plays. If you don't have the accompanying music for the book you can purchase it at realityofyourgreatness.com/music.

 Discussion Icon—This is the section where I share with you my personal insights into the Ray we are discussing. Think of it as you and I having a personal chat.

 Meditation Icon—This is the major exercise of the chapter. Since these meditations are designed to be between twenty to twenty-five minutes in duration, I highly recommend that you either read them into a recording device like your phone, or listen to them on the website at TheTwelveRays.com/meditations. There is no charge to access these recordings.

I hope these tools I've provided—this book, the meditations, and the music—will help you connect with each Ray and help you remember your connection to your whole self and believe in the reality of your greatness.

Michael S. L.

February 2018
Matthews, North Carolina

"It is time for you to choose your own condition, whether that be suffering and pain or joy and love, for Earth to choose to survive, or to LIVE, to live as a spiritual being, to draw the Spirit—the GOD of YOU—into this physical vessel, to know of the duality in your relative environment and to overcome, to choose the highest state of life within this environment.

"You have suffered. Is it not time for you to integrate, to BE what you have never been on this planet before, and to feel the joy and the opportunity that no other environment offers before it is destroyed by your own suffering?"

INTRODUCTION

You manifest in your being, in your emotional and physical makeup, that which you believe, that which you choose, that which you acquire through experience. But you can evolve that thought—that manifested thought—to create, elevate, morph, and change whatever you can believe to be true.

It is by choice that you have, as a human race, focused on discord, disease, [and] negativity, and your resurrection [is] dependent on a pattern change, a thought change, an empowerment.

What if you could grow rich just by thinking? Some people estimate the book *Think and Grow Rich* has sold over 60 million copies. As a matter of fact, there seems to be an entire personal and professional coaching industry built around the fundamental principal that "thoughts are things," which is a central premise of the book. What is there about thoughts that make them so valuable?

You can find several books that are titled *Thoughts Are Things*. One of the earliest ones that I found is by Prentice Mulford. It was written in 1889. Mulford states, "Our thought is the unseen magnet, ever attracting its correspondence in things seen and tangible" (page 136).

Bob Proctor and Greg Reid wrote a more recent book by that title in 2014. In case you are unfamiliar with Bob Proctor, he is the cofounder of the Proctor Gallagher Institute. According to the institute's website, Bob Proctor "is known as America's greatest prosperity teacher." Here is how Proctor and Reid describe the power of thought in their book: "Thoughts can generate monumental energy and produce results that were once perceived to be inconceivable. Thoughts have led to every invention and improvement known to humankind" (page 44).

Proctor worked side by side for many years with Earl Nightingale who wrote what many consider to be one of the great motivational books of all time, *Earl Nightingale's Greatest Discovery*. Here is what Wayne Dyer wrote in the foreword of that book: "Wow—the entire world wrapped up in those three magic words—THOUGHTS ARE THINGS! Think hard on this as you read the pages of Earl's book. A thought is the most powerful force in the universe. You can make your life whatever you wish if you learn to make your thoughts work for you" (page xvii).

I could go on and on with citations about how thoughts are things. When we learn to focus our attention, we can manifest anything in this physical dimension that we can imagine. It is often pointed out that this is exactly how innovation takes place. Someone uses their imagination to dream about something new like an airplane, a television, a computer, or a man standing on the Moon, and before too long, it is manifested into being.

Millions of people who bought Napoleon Hill's book seem to be willing to entertain the idea that you can think and grow rich. I wonder if they would be as interested in a book entitled *Think and Grow Healthy*. How about *Think and Feel Loved*? Do you believe you could think and eliminate pain and suffering in your life? If you have experienced any negativity in your life, do you think your thoughts have had anything to do with it? Why not believe that all of this is possible, and the time to experience it all is now?

I believe that thoughts are very powerful. Before anything can be brought into manifestation, it must first be conceived in thought. It is that ability to use our imaginations and conceive of something entirely new that enables us to create, take control of our own lives, and create our own realities. It is our heritage as part of what the authors mentioned above would describe as "Infinite Mind." I know it as the energy of the First Ray, the Ray of Divine Will.

But where does the power to manifest thoughts into reality really come from? What is the force in the universe that does all the heavy lifting when it comes to manifestation? Many refer to this as the Law of Attraction. The Law of Attraction was popularized by the 2006 movie *The Secret*. It received critical acclaim and reportedly earned $65 million. A book followed shortly and was on the *New York Times* best-seller list. The DVD version of the film was also a best seller. The movie featured interviews with over twenty-five prominent business people, teachers, and authors who all have promoted the Law of Attraction. Some of the above authors were featured in the movie.

If you have not heard about the Law of Attraction, it is basically the mechanism that allows thoughts to become things. It states that we attract to us what we are thinking. But again the question arises, how does the law work? In the physical world, when a scientist proclaims a law—say Newton's laws of motion—there is a description of what causes the law to be true. Sometimes there is no proof; there is only observation of the law as in the case of the law of gravity. It is assumed that understanding how the law works will come at some later time.

The Spiritualization of Success

"I have an opinion, and I don't think I'll ever get shaken off this. I believe if a program you're studying doesn't have a spiritual foundation, it is incomplete. It is incomplete, you're not going to win."
– BOB PROCTOR, *The Art of Living*

I have always sought to discuss the Rays in terms of everyday relevancy. I feel that in order for this information to have value to anyone, it must have practical applications. After I wrote the first draft of this book and before I committed to publishing it, I started work on a new project that had to do with Napoleon Hill's *Think and Grow Rich*. As I was doing my research, I came across numerous authors who had worked with the information in Hill's book and had become very successful as a result. Bob Proctor was one of those individuals.

The above quote struck me as very insightful. What was the spiritual foundation that all these methods were based upon? It seems to me that several of them, Hill's and Proctor's included, were based upon the spiritual teachings of the New Thought movement. It is not my intention to describe or promote the New Thought movement here. If you are interested in learning more about it, there are a variety of good books on the subject.

What occurred to me was that using the New Thought movement as the spiritual foundation, these authors could describe why their programs worked, but they could only go so far in describing how they worked. They can suggest you can be successful using the Law of Attraction, but they don't really explain how the Law of Attraction works.

My belief is that the Twelve Rays provide a framework for understanding the mechanisms that are behind some of these very fundamental laws. For example, the Law of Attraction is part of the Third Ray, the Ray of Active Intelligence. As you read this book, you will find a great deal of information about the Rays. Since these Rays come directly from the Source, or Infinite Intelligence, or All That Is, it should be clear that they represent the power behind the way things work. It is my intention to provide an additional layer of understanding about these "mysteries."

There are numerous accounts of individuals applying the Law of Attraction with little or no success. I agree whole-heartedly with Bob Proctor that any use of these "laws," any descriptions of processes to be followed, should be based on a solid spiritual foundation. Is there just one correct spiritual foundation? I really don't think so. What I do know is that as you learn about the Rays, as you work with them, you will begin to raise your energetic vibration. As you continue to raise your vibration, new knowledge will become available to you. You must do your own work, raise your own vibration, in order to successfully work with these "laws." You will be shown how to do this in the following chapters.

The first three Rays are your keys to a new way of personal creation and manifestation. They help you dare to imagine a higher vision of yourself. They remind you to create with love and wisdom, making sure that all you create is true to your own self. And they actively bring to you the resources necessary to manifest whatever you choose to experience in your life. All of this is part of our birthright as creations of the Creator, children of God. All of this is part of your Divine Heritage. Are you ready to create a grander version of yourself?

I believe understanding how the Law of Attraction works can be found in the Third Ray, the Ray of Active Intelligence. I believe this is the same energy that created all of this manifested reality, and I believe it flows through each and every one of us. It is also part of our heritage. We have the ability not only to imagine something new and different, as given by the First Ray, but also to manifest what we choose in this physical dimension by using the Third Ray energy.

The first three Rays are referred to as the Rays of Aspect. They are the aspects of our divine heritage. The Second Ray is called the Ray of Love and Wisdom. This Ray transmits Divine Love down through the dimensions of creation until it reaches our physical dimension. You may have heard the sayings God is love, there is only love, or all is love. I believe that all love comes from one Source and is filtered down to us here on Earth through the Second Ray. The Second Ray also communicates the wisdom that mankind uses to advance itself. There is much more discussion of these first three Rays in chapter 5.

The Clothing for the Energy That You Are

> *These Rays are a fine vibrational energy. And each Ray, each of these Twelve Rays, is filtered down from Source, through the cosmic realms, into your solar system and into Earth. They are truly the clothing for the energy that you are.*

We were all raised in a spiritual or religious tradition. Even no tradition is actually a kind of tradition. Many of these traditions have hardened into dogmas that resist change. If you feel that the world is a different place now than it was when these dogmatic religions were started, you may no longer find meaning in their messages. There is no specific spiritual foundation that is put forth in this book. I do, however, present several concepts that may be new to the reader. Perhaps they will help provide some clarity.

The Twelve Rays emanate from the Source, or All That Is. I was never taught about them in my early religious training. They are the energy behind the manifestation of all that we perceive in this physical dimension. They are the life force that animates manifested creation, and these energies are constantly flowing from the Source. You may have been taught that the universe was created some time ago, and since then it has been on its own. I agree that it began at some point. Allow me to suggest, however, that the universe is being constantly projected anew. You and I are being constantly projected anew. This is why change can sometimes be perceived as occurring instantaneously. Change can take place from moment to moment. This is one of those new concepts that I was referring to. You may not agree with me on this point, and that is alright. This is a personal belief I have come to after working with the Rays.

Many religious traditions teach about our relationship with God. Some of these traditions also teach about finding our way back to God through individual experience. There is often an emphasis on returning to something more elevated, more joyful and loving, more divine. But the emphasis is on returning.

The emphasis of the Twelve Rays is in the *other* direction. The Twelve Rays enable us to change things here on planet Earth. They provide the tools to elevate our experience here and now. What do I mean by elevate? I mean when we raise our own energetic levels—the frequencies that we vibrate at and exist on—we have more choices available to us. We can choose love over fear. We can choose joy over pain and suffering.

Of course, those choices are available to us right now, but many struggle with change. Joseph Campbell has written extensively about the great cultural myth that he refers to as the hero's journey. This journey involves a great deal of pain and suffering. He found the hero's journey narrative so prevalent in so many world cultures that he was able to stylize it into discrete phases. The hero's journey, no matter what version of the story you select, seems to have the same progression, the same flow. In the end of course, the hero is victorious, and everyone lives happily ever after most of the time.

Humankind has made pain and suffering so commonplace that it is easy to think it is normal. What if we were to view pain and suffering as a bad habit—a bad habit that we can now change? Are we ready to create a new myth about the hero's journey? Are we ready to create a hero who doesn't need to do battle with evil and defeat it? How about a hero who lives happily ever after by consciously creating his or her own reality?

It is time to replace the belief that spiritual progress is attained through pain and suffering with the understanding that spiritual growth is achieved through conscious creation. And conscious creation is achieved with grace and ease, through the expansion of your understanding of who you really are and recognition that resources of the universe are at your disposal. They are yours to command.

That is a radical statement of personal empowerment. What would it take to make that change and see yourself as a conscious creator? If only we had the right tools. But wait. Didn't I just say the Twelve Rays were about change?

The Twelve Rays allow each and every one of us to consciously become the creators of our own realities. We, of course, already do create our own realities with every choice we make. Every decision that we make shapes our personal realities. Our beliefs shape our perceptions of reality. No two individuals have the same personal reality.

The Twelve Rays help us to actually prepare our physical bodies to exist at higher energetic levels. The benefits of raising the energetic levels of our physical bodies—and actually the energetic levels of all of what we see manifested around us—are profound. Simply stated, these higher energetic vibrations afford us more choice for creating our personal experiences and personal realities than ever before.

The energy of the Twelve Rays flows through us. The Team refers to the Rays as "the clothing for the energy that you are." Most of us have forgotten that we can direct the energy of the Rays. Remember when you were a child and first learned to make drawings? You probably painted with your hands using finger paints and made images that were very basic shapes and forms. Perhaps you got some coloring books and used crayons to fill in the images that were already on the page. As you got older, you may have tried drawing with a pen or a pencil. Later, you may have tried paint by numbers and begun to understand how to make images out of shades of colors. Some may have progressed and learned more about brush strokes and perspective and begun to draw on blank canvases. And some artists become great masters. We all can become masters of the Twelve Rays.

Most of us don't really notice how much control we have over our personal realities. The Twelve Rays help us to take conscious control of our choices and thereby enable us to become conscious creators. This doesn't happen overnight for most of us. It takes work and dedication to become a master.

The Twelve Rays are tools to help us connect with the larger aspects of our personal consciousness, and when we do, we can change the nature of our experience here on this planet. We can use the Twelve Rays to experience what has never before been available to experience—new insights and new awareness. Does that sound almost too good to be true? We are in a time of great change. We have the choice to make the changes or to keep going the way we have been going. Now we have the tools to help us if we decide to make the changes.

As you work with the Rays, as you build up your personal energetic level, you open to this new potential, this new way of being.

Why Now?

When the Team presented information about the Twelve Rays, one thing became clear for me: this is a time of great change, a time for new awareness. Up until the time when I received this information, I had been aware of the first seven Rays, but I really didn't understand their usefulness. Then the Team presented all twelve, the original seven plus the Rays of Soul Integration (Rays Eight through Twelve). They explained how the Rays provide a clear path to raising personal energetic levels. The Rays are given at this time to help individuals participate in the changes that involve us all. They are particularly meant to help each of us evolve our own personal consciousness.

One of the most exciting, new aspects of working with the Rays is found in the higher Rays, the Rays of Soul Integration. When you work with these higher Rays, you have the opportunity to bring a larger part of your soul-level consciousness into this dimension. That is what soul integration is all about. As you begin to do this, you raise your own personal energetic vibrations as well as the energetic vibration of the entire planet. We are all connected.

The information provided by the Team and the guided journeys included here provide clear and easy-to-follow techniques for working with these higher Rays. Those guided journeys are included within each chapter and are also available to you in audio format at TheTwelveRays.com. Through the use of these techniques, you will be prepared for and be able to open to new insights and awareness.

It is your choice to participate or not, and we all have free will. If you are ready to move forward, then you will find a great deal of useful information in the following pages. My hope is that you will begin to understand the opportunity that awaits each and every one of us who is ready to embrace the energy of the Twelve Rays.

I often refer to the Rays as a metaphor. They represent a context in which to have an orderly discussion on a topic that most of us can't really perceive with our physical senses and our human brains just yet. But the more we work with this metaphor, the better we get at directing the Rays and realizing the benefits they offer all humankind. I believe that real understanding of the Rays is beyond our current ability to perceive. So we work with the metaphor as it is with the intention to make it as real as possible for us.

Reincarnation

You don't have to believe in reincarnation to benefit from the Twelve Rays. If you already believe in an eternal soul, then you believe that you are currently incarnated. The concept of repeated life experiences, reincarnation, is just whether you believe you've incarnated more than once. If you do believe in reincarnation or are at least open to exploring it, then the benefits of working with the Twelve Rays become even more relevant to you.

These repeated life experiences tend to accumulate a fair amount of reincarnational baggage—emotional and otherwise—that sooner or later need to be transmuted into higher energetic forms. The Seventh and Eighth Rays are especially suited to handle such energetic transformations.

I have encountered numerous individuals who believe that they are on a final segment of some reincarnational cycle, and they feel a need to transmute lifetimes worth of baggage. The Rays are well suited to this task.

There is also a belief held by many that the beliefs you die with are the beliefs you are born with in the next incarnation. In a sense, the final part of a current lifetime becomes a foundation for the next lifetime. If you believe that might be the case, then using the higher Rays to connect with your whole self will enable personal perspectives and beliefs that you have quite literally never been able to access before. Using the Rays to raise your personal energetic vibration in this lifetime affords access to levels of understanding and perceptions that have not been available until now. You can literally lay the foundation for an entirely new set of life experiences.

How to Read This Book

This book more or less follows my journey—the sequence in which I received the information about the Rays. It has been many years since I first received this information, and my understanding of the Rays has deepened over time. For each Ray then, after I share with you my initial experience, I'll give you my current understanding of the Rays under the heading of "discussion." In some cases, my understanding of the Rays that I am presenting under the discussion heading has evolved substantially over time.

Over the last several years, I have developed and taught several seminars on the Twelve Rays. I generally structured each class so that there would be an informative introduction and then an experiential portion. I created guided meditations for each class to help the participants connect more personally with the energy of the Rays. These meditations are included here also to help you connect with the Rays. You can simply read them into a personal recording device like your phone and then relax and play it back, or you can go to TheTwelveRays.com and listen for free as I indicated previously.

There is a worksheet included after each meditation. These are there for your use. Make use of them as you see fit. It has been my experience that often the experiences and insights that one gets during these meditations quickly slip away, much like they do in dreams. The worksheets are provided to help you record what you just experienced so that you will have it as reference.

There is also a short summary of key concepts. Information is just that—information. I've read so many books, and it seems that as soon as I finish one, another appears. Where do all of those valuable insights go? I believe they need to be processed. What I mean by that is they need to be converted from information into wisdom. I define wisdom as knowledge combined with personal experience and personal beliefs. Each summary sheet will have the key information that was presented and then the integrated wisdom that I hope it leads you to.

You have a choice: you can either read this book and not take the time to personally experience each Ray, moving on to your next piece of reading when you are finished; or you can work with the Rays, experience them as they resonate with you, and reap the benefit of these unlimited, divine energies. Let me be clear: there is no right or wrong way to work with the Rays. Work with them as you choose. Find what works best for you.

Now I would like to introduce you to the Team.

First Things First

"Our message is very simple. We have expressed it many times. Coming into this relative world in this physical body, you were a cup of energy with boundaries that you set up as you entered this world. It is time to overflow the glass and expand your boundaries and understand what fills that cup and how it can exist beyond the boundaries that were set when you first moved into this environment."

CHAPTER 1

The Team

Who is the Team? I could give you names, and their names are certainly known to most of us in the west. Humans really enjoy giving labels to things. It is part of our communication training. Most of the time, this type of labeling is actually beneficial because it helps clarify what we are talking about. But labels, just like names, are limiting. And as William Shakespeare wrote, "What's in a name? That which we call a rose by any other name would smell as sweet."

Having said that, their names are recognizable, and if I were to release them, then you would immediately associate any prior information you might have regarding those names to the members of the Team. That would be limiting because they are not interacting with us based solely on their earthly experiences or the historical accounts of their lives.

They share their perspectives with us, which is a different perspective than we currently have. And as they share that different perspective, it allows us to think differently about our experiences, beliefs, and goals. When we see things from a different perspective, all kinds of new possibilities present themselves. Our choices expand, and we are free to choose things that we never before thought were possible choices.

Their perspective and the way they construct concepts may take some getting used to. I am tempted to rewrite some of their conversation to make it clearer. If I were to change their words, however, I am afraid the depth would be lost. Instead, I will add my own words to provide my interpretation of their meaning. I find that when I reread the sessions later, I often put words and ideas together differently than before, and this allows me to have a different perspective on what I thought they were originally saying.

I met Julie about a year before we started working directly with the Team. She was a frequent participant in a couple of the ongoing meetings we sponsored at the wellness facility that I owned at the time. Julie and I began working directly with the Team in 2005, and we still work with them today. They are, needless to say, not from around here. Julie is a trance medium, which means that when we communicate with the Team, she goes into a trance, and they speak through her. Most of the time, Julie has little or no recollection of the conversation.

Julie and I have spoken often about her experience during the sessions. While it is true that most of the time she has no memory of what she is saying, she nevertheless plays the most vital role as the receiver of the information. As best as I can understand it, she receives the information in a multisensory manner. She then translates the information into words. The Team is not actually speaking English words to her. They are communicating information that she converts into words.

Sessions generally start out with the Team talking to me, and I just sit there and listen. I never really know what they are going to talk about. Then there is a question-and-answer part where I get to ask any questions that I choose. We record these sessions, and I transcribe them afterward. That is when Julie gets to read what was discussed during the session.

The Team works with us on many levels. They help us to stay focused on our goals. They encourage us to remember what we already know but have limited our access to—where we came from and the nature of our true existence. They provide us information that we share with others. They do all that and more to help us accomplish what we came here to do.

The Team explained how they would present the information about the Rays to us so that we would have time to integrate them. I have followed that same format in presenting the information here. This is what they shared with us:

> *We wish to acknowledge your interest in understanding each individual energy Ray. We are aware of your interest in pursuing more knowledge. Yet the time has not been right. When it is, very soon, as with our guidance up to this point, you will be given the experience of each Ray, one at a time, so that you may integrate fully its energy.*
>
> *For us to hand you this information only through voice and language would not serve as would the experience of integrating each Ray—a single Ray—one at a time.*

I have followed their lead and presented the Rays individually throughout the book.

The Plan

Do you feel that there is purpose to your life? Or do you feel that life is random, and you are just living day to day? There are many individuals who don't remember that they are here with intention. They don't believe that they are more than this particular experience they are having in this particular lifetime. They don't remember how splendid their existence is beyond this dimension. Life can be very confusing with its many turns and twists. Why are we here? If you were to randomly ask individuals why they are here, my bet would be that most don't have a clue why they are here.

Then why are we here? My short answer to that question is to carry on the act of creation. We are here to continue to create through our experiences and our choices. We are free to create heaven or hell here in this dimension, on this planet. It seems to me that we have a great deal of experience in making life a living hell. I for one am ready for a change.

When we decide to have an experience here on Earth, my belief is that it is well planned out. I think of it as much like going on a road trip. You begin by establishing certain objectives. Seeing the Grand Canyon would be very nice—then perhaps a side trip to Flagstaff, Arizona. Good. I have established a primary and a secondary objective. Now I must decide how I am going to travel there. Should I fly or drive? Well, this depends really on how much time I want to spend on the way, on the journey. Am I in a hurry, or can I take my time?

Another consideration is will I travel alone, or will I ask some friends to join me? Then there is the packing to consider. What time of year is it? What type of weather do I anticipate along the way, and what will it be like when I arrive at my destination? When I get there, will I camp out or stay in a hotel? You can see I am putting quite a bit of planning into this journey.

We do the same thing when we plan our next experience here on Earth. What objectives do I want to set for myself? Most people plan for many possible objectives. Who will I journey with? What is the best family experience to get me headed in the right direction? What personality traits will help me to achieve my objectives? How much time am I going to take, and which time period is best suited for me and this experience? Which culture offers the best potentials to achieve my goals? All of these considerations and more go into planning an incarnation.

It is rather easy for me to accept the validity of reincarnation. You see, I have been chatting with the Team for several years, and it is clear to me that they exist in a realm beyond this dimension. Their individual and collective consciousness are not restricted to the limitations of this dimension. As you read our conversations, I believe you will get to know them and appreciate that their perspective of reality is far different than ours here in this dimension.

The members of the Team are our friends who agreed to support us in this current experience. They remind us of who we really are and where we really come from. They remind us that we are on a journey that is well thought out and has intention. What is the intention for our journey? That is the fun of it. The intention of our journey is ours to discover. Julie and I know our coming together is a significant part of that intention. We know that remembering who we are and where we came from is critical to the completion of our intentions.

The Team constantly supports us along our journey. Sometimes that support is in the form of information like the Twelve Rays. Sometimes it is in the form of reassurance. It is comforting to know that you are not alone no matter how strong the illusion of aloneness may seem. Sometimes they challenge us to work harder. They always surround us with their love and remind us that Divine Love is the most powerful force in all of creation and beyond.

I didn't always embrace the notion of being a multidimensional being. I rigorously resisted the notion of reincarnation in fact. I often pondered the concept of life after death. After all, that was my religious upbringing. I was never really comfortable, for some unknown reason, with the idea of living in heaven with God for all eternity. Seems odd, but that notion was never easy for me to embrace. I found it to be quite satisfactory to defer any further thinking on the matter. Then I was introduced to the Team, and that changed everything for me.

Let's talk about your team. Have you ever considered the possibility that you have a team just like ours? If you haven't, then I suggest you consider the possibility that you set up a support team before you incarnated into this experience, just like Julie and I did. Some may be familiar with the concepts of spirit guides and teachers. This is pretty much the same idea. If you have connected with your team or your guides and teachers or your angels or whatever name you give them, then you know how much help and assistance is available to you in this lifetime.

If you haven't yet connected with your friends whom you left behind when you came into this lifetime, then I suggest you make the effort to open to them. You will be well rewarded. You are not alone. You have never been alone. But the illusion of being alone can be very strong as I mentioned earlier. In the next chapter, there is a lovely guided meditation, which I use to help individuals connect with their friends who are not in this dimension with them. I call it the Bridge Meditation, and it is a very nice and relaxing way to open to the support your guides and teachers—your team—are waiting to provide you.

The Twelve Rays will be discussed in great detail in the remainder of this book. The important concept to talk about at the beginning of our discussion is that the last five Rays, Rays Eight through Twelve, have only recently become available to us here on Earth to work with. Why are they available now? Because it is a time *of* change, a time *to* change. These Rays are tools to help us in our transformation.

Some scholars estimate that as many as 240 million people died in the twentieth century as a result of war and other man-made disasters. The twentieth century can rightfully be called the bloodiest century humankind has ever experienced. There is no need to continue things the way they are, and there should be every reason in the world to try something different. The Rays are offered as tools for personal transformation because the only way to change the world is by changing yourself.

Many of us are not comfortable with change. It seems quite a paradox that many of us strive to maintain the status quo when everything around us is really in a state of change. So let's consider personal change management in the next section.

CHAPTER 2

Managing Personal Change

The Team often talks about fear and the impact it has on us. I would like to share an insightful comment from them as we begin this section on managing personal change.

> *If there were no fear of change, there would be very little fear. Stop focusing on fear and start teaching of the power. You have an inscription that reminds you, "What would you do if you were unafraid?" "How much would you do if you knew you could not fail?" "What would you be if you knew you could be anything?" Inspire. Neutralize the fear. Empower.*

The inscriptions the Team refers to hang on the walls in my office. They are reminders to let go of our past patterns. They challenge us to think in new ways, and I believe they encourage us to step into our power. Resistance to change is very powerful. I often ponder why this is, and part of the answer is provided by the recent, exciting research in neuroplasticity.

When we do something over and over, it creates habituated patterns in our brains. We create neural pathways that are actually shortcuts of a sort. We really don't have to think about how to respond because we have responded in the same way so often. It becomes a habit. This results not only in doing the same actions repeatedly but also in thinking the same thoughts and coming to the same conclusions.

Here is the exciting news: researchers are finding that our brains can actually create new neural pathways that help us adapt to changes in our personal environments. We create these new neural pathways by making new and different choices that replace the old patterns. With time, the old patterns fall into disuse and disconnect themselves.

Perhaps another part of the answer of why change is so hard lies in our denial of our true identities as multidimensional beings. We often see ourselves as limited, as having limited abilities and resources. We see ourselves as our stories. It is time to remember that we are more than our stories. We are more than this particular experience that we are currently having. It is time to have a new relationship with change.

As we begin to work with the Twelve Rays, it is necessary to release our fears about change and embrace change for the reality that it is. Change promotes progress, and that is the essence of what we are experiencing now. You can learn how to manage change, and you can learn to manage it with grace and ease. Like most things, it gets easier with practice.

When you work with the energies of the Rays, it is more than likely that things will begin to shift for you. It is often hard to notice change within ourselves. That is why the people around us are often the first ones to comment on the shifts they see in our behavior. More than just being observers, they often have a vested interest in keeping things the way they are, in maintaining the status quo.

Many of our relationships, especially the longer-term ones, have a codependent characteristic to them. These types of relationships have implicit bargains or agreements in them. I'll give you this if you give me that in return. Think about it for a minute. You most certainly have that type of arrangement with your employer, and there is nothing wrong with that. You provide a certain amount of work in a given period of time, and the employer provides you with income in some form or another.

Now think about your personal relationships. If you have a spouse, is there an agreement that you supply this and get that in return? Most likely there is. I bring this to the marriage or relationship, and you supply that. I'll earn the income, and you take care of the kids and the house. I know that sounds pretty outdated, but many of us were raised in families like that. These days, it is more like we both contribute to the household income, and we both look after the kids and the household.

But what happens when something changes? What happens when the third child comes, and the mother wants to stay home with all the children? What happens when one of the partners spends too much time on the Internet? What if the sports enthusiast wants to spend more time on the golf course or at the tennis court? Then there is an interest in renegotiating the agreement.

This is where the trouble can begin. One partner wants to maintain the status quo, and the other is looking for a change. Or perhaps one of the partners doesn't even recognize that the terms of the original agreement have changed. This wasn't part of the deal, or I didn't bargain for this, the status quo proponent asserts. In order to come to a new agreement, both parties have to be agreeable to the new terms. Even when general agreement is reached, in most cases, only time will tell if the new agreement satisfies both parties.

What about your parents? When you were little you certainly had a codependent relationship with them. Is it still that way? How about your friends? Is there codependency in those relationships? A great way to tell is to start changing and see how they adjust to the new you. Most friends and relatives will be quick to tell you if they are OK with your changes. This is one of the most fundamental challenges to personal change that exists. The environment around us is vested in maintaining the status quo. When they see the changes in us, they want to help us to see the error in our ways so that we can shift back to the way things were. Or perhaps they are willing to encourage us to change our behaviors or our beliefs but only if they conform to their ideas of right and wrong.

This is quite a normal response, and we should not think that they are trying to hold us back as much as they are trying to keep things the same, the way they think things should be. This presents a number of fine opportunities to chat with our friends and relatives in a loving way. Some will support you, and some will be fearful of the change. This is part of the process. As you go through this process, keep in mind the golden rule—do to others what you want them to do to you. Treat them with love and respect and ask them to do the same with you.

One of the most difficult aspects of experiencing spiritual growth when you work with the Rays is that you notice that you are changing and everyone else is staying the same. Just as they have to love you in such a way as to allow for your personal growth, you would do well to reciprocate and love them in such a way that it is OK for them to pursue their lives' paths as they see best, even if that means staying where they are. It is not for us to judge what is best for someone else, and indeed losing judgment of others is hopefully one of the insights that you have gained along the way.

Still, there is something about human nature that motivates us to want to share our good experiences. When we gain valuable insight into the nature of reality, we naturally want to share it with others so that they too can benefit from this new awareness. Many of us have tried that only to experience resistance, and resistance is to be expected. If you share some particular personal revelation with a friend, you might notice that it doesn't have the same profound impact on him or her as it had on you.

Experience is always personal, and we all interpret information and events in our own unique ways. The insight you gain from a particular moment of clarity might lead to a vastly different experience for one of your friends. Still, sharing is good. Just don't be too attached to the reaction of the person you are sharing with.

The Multidimensional Self

One of the significant insights that is available to anyone who works with the Rays is that you are a multidimensional being. Once you embrace that concept, you can move from a mental understanding that you are a multidimensional being to a visceral experience of what it means to be a multidimensional being. What do I mean by this? The concept of existing in multiple dimensions might seem to make sense to you, but so what? What difference does knowing that make to the way you are experiencing your life? It is often difficult if not impossible to determine if anyone else on the planet thinks the same way you do. Does anyone else really see themselves as a multidimensional being?

Turn on the television and watch the evening shows. It is hard to conceive that most people are only interested in reality and detective shows or in comedy shows with prerecorded laugh tracks, but that is what is generally on mainstream television channels. And by the way, I find the repetitive nature of the commercials to be quite mind-numbing. What good does it do to think of yourself as any different than your neighbor?

In reality, you are not any different than your neighbor. You are, however, having a different experience of life than your neighbor, and that is significant. As a matter of fact, you are having a unique experience of life. No one else on the planet is experiencing life the same way that you are. And that is a good thing.

Let's get back to the question—what good does it do you to believe you are a multidimensional being having this experience in this single dimension? If your goal is to just get through this experience with as little pain and suffering as possible, then that understanding of your multidimensional self is probably of not much value and has presumably little practical impact on your life. But what if you want more out of life? What if you feel there is more to experience or a different way to achieve your goals? This is where that understanding of your multidimensional nature really comes in handy.

The perspective of existing in multiple dimensions simultaneously encourages you to seek out the purpose you set for this life experience before you ever entered this dimension. This perspective allows you to know that you have everything, every tool and constant support, all available to you. It allows you to step into your own power as a cocreator of this dimension. It allows you to be successful at whatever you choose to accomplish. Here is where the Rays are so helpful. They help you move from just knowing this about yourself to actually being able to embrace this knowledge of your multidimensional beingness and use it to create your reality here, now, in this life experience on this planet.

Let's just for a moment suggest that part of your life's plan is to help everyone on the planet move out of this mindset of pain and suffering and to move forward to a reality of experiencing life through grace and ease. What if that was of interest to you? You would want to know how you could accomplish such a challenge. The answer is really quite simple. You change yourself. You lead by example. You become the change you want to see. Sound familiar? There's nothing new here. We have heard this all before. The work that you do on yourself helps all of us move forward, and that is spectacular.

Even if you don't think you set such an altruistic goal for yourself in this lifetime, the shift that happens in you is felt by everyone around you. If you are shifting your energy and lifting yourself to a higher level of consciousness, everyone around will notice. Your shift in and of itself is helping to move us all in the right direction. It is helping us all to move out of this habit of fear and suffering. Just by being yourself, you show others that they have a choice. They can stay where they are, or they can choose something new.

The work that you do, the internal work that we will focus on throughout this entire book, benefits everyone. That is why it is so important. That is why you are so important.

You probably will not learn how to manage this internal change overnight. You will, however, get better and better at it over time.

The Bridge Meditation I mentioned earlier is multipurpose. I encourage you to work with it often and to try different variations to help you identify the areas of yourself that need work.

The first objective in working with the Bridge Meditation should be to make contact with your support team. Sometimes we refer to them as your guides and your teachers. Some may choose to call them your angels. The labels aren't really important. Pick something that works for you. Connect with your helpers and allow yourself to be surrounded by their love. You will surely feel it if you allow yourself to. Once you have made contact with them or perhaps if you already have made contact, you will find them to be very helpful in working with the Rays.

Here is a general recommendation for all the meditations in this book: read through each meditation completely before doing it. Then you can proceed using your memory alone. If this doesn't work very well for you, then let me suggest that you read the meditation into a recording device of some sort like your phone. All these meditations are also available to listen to free of charge on my web site at TheTwelveRays.com. Here is the Bridge Meditation. Work with it and see how much you can open to.

 ## The Bridge Meditation

Arrange your feet either flat on the floor or comfortably tucked underneath you. Allow your hands to rest comfortably in your lap or at your sides, whichever feels more comfortable to you.

Let's begin with a gentle deep breath. Focus your awareness on your relaxed breathing. Allow it to become nice and rhythmic. Keeping your awareness focused on your gentle, relaxed breathing, imagine that each time you breathe in, you breathe in a nice fresh breath of relaxation. And with each exhale you breathe out any stress or tension. That's right, breathing in relaxation and releasing stress and tension with each exhale.

See yourself walking along a beautiful country path that runs alongside a crystal-clear mountain stream. The sun is shining, and you can feel its warmth. As you continue to walk, you can feel the coolness of the morning air brush against your face. You are surrounded by pristine countryside. There is no one else around. You continue to walk along this path, and as you do, you notice the beautiful trees in full bloom. You notice the deep colors of the flowers that bloom all around creating nature's lush palette of color.

As you continue to walk, you notice a bridge up ahead. You continue to walk, getting closer and closer to the bridge, and now you come to the bridge. I'd like you to begin to cross over the bridge. When you get to the middle of the bridge, I'd like you to pause and take a step to the side and look underneath the bridge. If you see water, notice if the water is clear or cloudy. Notice if you can see anything in it or on it. Notice if it is flowing at all, and if it is flowing, is it flowing quickly or slowly? If you see something else that is totally fine. Just notice. Good.

Now take a step back and notice the bridge. Just look at the bridge. What shape is it? Is it flat or arched or perhaps some other shape? What size is it? Is it big enough for just one person or is it bigger? And what is it made out of? Perhaps it is made out of stone or metal or wood or perhaps some other material. Just observe the bridge.

Now continue to cross the bridge until you reach the other side. On the other side, you see a path that goes off into the countryside. Follow the path and, as you do, allow the landscape to take any shape you wish. You may see beautiful snow-capped mountains or perhaps low rolling hills or maybe just lush grasslands. There may be crystal-clear mountain lakes, or perhaps you are at the beach and can see the ocean with the waves flowing in. Now look up into the sky as you walk and look at the deep blue sky. Perhaps you see beautiful, fluffy clouds. Maybe you see big birds flying back and forth. Perhaps you can see other animals in the distance or maybe even close up.

As you continue to walk and take in the beautiful panorama of the Creator's handiwork, you notice in the distance a fork in the road. As you get closer you realize that you must choose to go either to the left or to the right. Now you come to that fork, and you choose to continue either to the left or to the right. And as you continue to walk, you begin to feel very relaxed and at ease. This path looks familiar to you, and indeed it is very familiar to you. You have come this way many, many times before. You feel safe and secure.

The path now leads you into a clearing, and as you enter, you recognize this place. You recognize this place as your sacred place, a place you have been to many, many times. This is where you come to meet with your guides and your teachers. You come here to get guidance and to connect with all those who support you in this journey, this experience you are having.

Now look around and find a comfortable place to sit or lie down. You may see a chair or perhaps a tree trunk or a log or maybe even a stone. Or maybe you just want to lie down in the grass. Do whatever feels right. Just relax and get comfortable.

Now call in your guides and teachers to be with you. Allow yourself, in this altered state of awareness, to feel their love for you. Allow yourself to be surrounded by their love. If you have a desire to speak with a particular entity, go ahead now and ask that entity to come forward. Perhaps there is a particular question for which you are seeking guidance. Whatever the purpose or intention, now is the time. Perhaps you have a particular purpose for your journey today; go ahead now and complete your intention. I'll give you some time to yourself and your guides and teachers.

(Wait two minutes.)

In a minute, we will begin our journey back. Take this remaining time to finish up whatever it is that you are doing.

(Wait one minute.)

Now as we prepare to return, stand up and exchange your final farewells to all who have joined you today. When you are ready, turn and find the path that leads back. Now begin to walk back along the path, and as you do, bring back with you all the memories that you have from your experience today.

Now you reach the place where the path comes back together again. And as you continue to walk you look around again at the landscape and just notice if it is the same as you remember or if it has changed at all. Just simply notice. As you continue to walk and notice the beautiful scenery, you notice the bridge up ahead. And as you continue to walk, you get closer and closer to the bridge until finally you reach the bridge.

I'd like you to begin to cross back over the bridge. When you get to the middle of the bridge, I'd like you to pause and take a step to the side and look underneath the bridge. Again, if you see water, notice if the water is clear or cloudy. Notice if you can see anything in it or on it. Notice if it is flowing at all, and if it is flowing, is it flowing quickly or slowly? If you see anything other than water, that is perfectly fine. Just notice. Good.

Now take a step back and notice the bridge once again. Just look at the bridge. What shape is it? Is it the same as before or perhaps some other shape? What about the size? Is it the same as it was? And what is it made out of? Is it still made of the same material? Just observe the bridge.

Now continue to walk back across the bridge, and when you come to the other side, you once again notice the path that runs alongside the beautiful mountain stream. Follow the path back to the place where you began. And when you reach that place, I would like you to take a gentle, deep breath, and as you breathe nice and rhythmically, allow your consciousness to begin to return to your physical body. And as your consciousness begins to return to your physical body, gently move your fingers and your toes. And as you move your fingers and your toes, begin to reconnect with your arms and your legs. Now allow your consciousness to fully return to your body, and when you are ready, gently open your eyes and return to this place and this time. Welcome back.

You can use this meditation in a number of different ways. The more you work with it, the easier it will be to improvise when you reach your sacred place.

Bridge Meditation

INSIGHTS

You will find the following worksheet really valuable to help put the experience you just had into a usable format. The time you spend in journaling your experience will pay off handsomely for you.

Insights: list as many as you can remember.

_____

_____

_____

_____

Main concepts: what is the subject matter behind the concepts?

_____

_____

_____

Meaning for you: how do you interpret these insights?

_____

_____

_____

_____

How can you use this in your daily life?

_____

_____

_____

Why is that helpful?

_____

_____

_____

Bridge Meditation FAQs

To help you get more out of this particular meditation, I've prepared a short list of frequently asked questions that I hope will provide you with some additional explanations.

Is the water under the bridge symbolic?

Generally water is thought of as being symbolic of our emotions. So swiftly moving water suggests that a lot of emotions are currently flowing. Slowly moving water could be considered an indication that your emotions are pretty steady. The visibility of the water could point to the source of the water condition. Cloudy or murky water might mean that you are unclear as to the source of these emotions. Objects in or on the water have their own meaning best determined by you. Pay attention to whether the water is the same on the way over and the way back across. Make a mental note of any differences you notice.

What significance is the shape and construction of the bridge?

You are the best person to determine the meaning of the symbols in your meditation. Is your bridge constructed from strong, durable material, or is it fragile and in need of repair? Is it difficult to cross, or does it feel safe and light? Does it change after spending time with your guides? Does the bridge appear different on the way back from the visit with your guides?

Does it make a difference if I choose the right or the left path to follow?

Yes, indeed it does. But only you know which path is the correct path for you to choose today. There are no wrong choices since either path leads you to one of your sacred places. You may even come to the fork in the road and see more than two paths. These are choices that give you opportunity to empower yourself. From meditation to meditation you can continue to select the same path or choose differently. Be curious to explore the different pathways.

What if I don't recognize my sacred place?

Trust in the process. You may not be a visual person. If it doesn't look familiar to you, try sensing the energy of the place. How did you feel when you reached your sacred place? If you are not a visual person, can you hear any sounds or sense an energy shift?

What if I call on my guides and teachers, and no one shows up?

Your guides and your teachers always show up. You may have a hard time sensing their presence at first. Relax—don't try to force it. The easiest way to sense them is to let go of any preconceived ideas of how they will reveal themselves to you. They may be sensed as energy or light, animals, colors, sounds, or even smells. Be as open as possible.

Should I always have a question ready to ask?

It is always a good idea to have a question prepared when you begin the meditation. Be very clear in your questions and in the type of answer you are requesting. Your guides exist in a more expansive dimension without judgment. The more precise you can be in your questions, the more precisely your guides will answer. I believe your questions are already known to your guides and teachers. They may wait for you to ask in order to honor your free will. Sometimes you may not be open to accept the answer they bring, so you disregard the input you sense. If you cannot think of a specific question, ask them to provide you with some of their wisdom that is appropriate for you at that time.

Sometimes they come to you bearing a gift. If this happens, then focus on their intention rather than your own. You will find that what they bring is indeed for your highest and best good.

What happens if I forget what happened during the meditation?

This rarely happens. If it does, don't worry about it. You have received the message, and your subconscious mind still remembers it. You may be reminded in a dream later that evening, or you may receive the same message again in another meditation.

It seems like I made this entire experience up in my mind. Is any of it real?

It's all real. Sometimes the messages we receive are not the ones we were expecting. So we immediately go into denial mode. Take some time and let the new information settle in.

What if my mind drifts with images different from the guided journey?

Go with whatever you imagine. Each experience will be unique. For example, in the guided meditation I may say you are walking "down" a path when you sense your path floating "up." That's fine. Let your path take you where you need to go. Allow your inner vision and guidance to show you what is appropriate. And enjoy!

How can I remember the symbols and messages I receive?

I suggest you write down the symbols and messages. Sometimes what you receive will make more sense to you weeks or months after receiving them. Having them to reference will help you understand the process of communicating with wisdom far greater than ours. Writing down the symbols will help you compare what is happening in your life to the images received. You might even make a note about what is happening in your life compared to the message received. Messages can often be received on many levels, so what you cannot understand today may make beautiful sense in a week or month or year from now.

CHAPTER 3

Introduction to the Rays

Some might think that a book about the Twelve Rays might be a little too far out there, perhaps a bit too metaphysical or maybe something for individuals with psychic abilities. It might be hard to imagine how working with the Twelve Rays could be at all practical. After all, we all have to get up in the morning and go about our daily business whether that is looking after a family, going to work, or perhaps doing both. How can a working knowledge of the Rays help with that?

I see the Rays as being part of my spiritual life, and I see my spiritual life as part of my personal and professional lives, and all that makes me who I am. I see the Rays as not being too far out but part of how I integrate Spirit into my daily life.

We hear so much talk these days about the body-mind-spirit connection. Spirit for me is not something that I just concern myself with on Sunday mornings. Spirit for me is not defined by dogma. It is not something that was given thousands of years ago in the past. It is alive and active in my life. I see Spirit all around me. I see it in nature when I behold a beautiful landscape or am fortunate enough to observe a sunset with breathtaking hues of violet, red, orange, and yellow. I see it in the eyes of a baby or in the face of a child at play or in the embrace of a loving couple. I feel Spirit in my heart when I connect with love.

The energy of the Rays is the energy of love. It is the life force that animates all of creation. We tend to keep our focus on things that we can perceive most readily with our physical senses. So many of us have underutilized our nonphysical senses. Spirit moves just as vibrantly in the unseen realms of creation as it does in the manifested realms. There are many techniques given in the following chapters to help you connect to the Rays and utilize them in whatever manner you choose. They are all available to each and every person. I use them to bring Spirit into my everyday life, and what a difference that makes.

Here is the first conversation Julie and I had with the Team about the Twelve Rays. There are many more conversations that follow. Please keep in mind that I often either say things or ask questions during these sessions. The Team's comments are presented in italics. Mine are in roman. This first session starts off with me speaking.

Today is Thursday, July 14, 2005. We greet and welcome our Team, and we ask they continue to instruct us in the cosmic laws.

The Twelve Rays that illuminate and create the light substance in your Earth come from an undifferentiated Source.

What kind of a source?

Undifferentiated—ALL BEING—All One. And they are a fine vibrational energy. And each Ray, each of these Twelve Rays—they are filtered down from Source, through the cosmic realms, into your solar system, and into Earth—[is] truly the clothing for the energy that you are. Each Ray perfect unto itself. Each Ray an aspect—whole yet focused on individual aspects, lit by the light from transformational fire of pure-white light, blending and creating life as you know it in your dimension, creating what ultimately becomes your spiritual body, sending out Rays beyond your physical being, a finer, softer, lighter energy sometimes called your aura or your etheric body, storing all action from your physical life and those in-between, storing all that serves you.

And all that causes you discomfort builds in this energy, manifesting in the physical body, becoming dense if not cleansed, becoming pain and illness. This is why you may feel the discomfort outside the physical body that accumulates in the energy. It creates vortexes of energy. It blocks the flow. It works to shut down the free-flowing effect, the infinite reserve from Source.

We wish that you are to know these energies—to know that they exist—these new energies, these new Rays available like never before, as tools to help you heal, to help you integrate the God that you are into this physical vessel.

May I ask about the Twelve Rays please? I am familiar with the Seven Rays as have been described in the works of Alice Bailey and that generally we called the ancient wisdom and esoteric Christianity. Do the Twelve Rays that you're talking about include those Seven Rays and add on five additional ones?

There are five—five additional that are a blending of the lower seven.

And do they correspond to the five new chakras also?

They are not chakra oriented, although there is a connection. The blending of the top five [the Rays of Soul Integration], the additional five is the beginning of your integration, your soul blending with your physical being, a blending of your emotional and mental bodies as never before. It is energy that works with an individual to bring you closer into awareness and understanding of the reality of your greatness and works with your planet, as your planet breathes, integrating its oneness to the dimension that it resides in and the other dimensions that await to be realized in its awakening. It works within your solar system with the life force of your galaxy. And it works with each cell, with each heart center, creating new life at ALL levels. It is an endless reservoir creating and cleansing and creating NEW.

The Rays that we speak of are not chakra Rays; they are the Rays of Creation and Transformation.

Then why are they available to us now?

Your world is changing. It is the energy that is available that makes this change, and it is the opening from higher wisdom that it has allowed this energy to flow. Your world is at a crucial point, and these energies are offered, as our wisdom is offered to you, for you to draw that part of it into your beingness, into Earth's beingness, to create as never before, to rise, to shine, to transcend your limits, to heal yourself. Are you not ready?

We are ready. But perhaps there is more work to do.

It is time for you to choose your own condition, whether that be suffering and pain or joy and love, for Earth to choose to survive, or to LIVE, to live as a spiritual being, to draw the Spirit—the GOD of YOU—into this physical vessel, to know of the duality in your relative environment and to overcome, to choose the highest state of life within this environment.

You have suffered. Is it not time for you to integrate, to BE what you have never been on this planet before, and to feel the joy and the opportunity that no other environment offers before it is destroyed by your own suffering?

Call us when you need our help and encouragement or feel you "can't"—you can't on your own. Just call on us. Know that you have our love. We are never far. You are God. Honor us by letting your light shine!

It is now ten years later, and when I read these words, I still find new meaning in them. I suspect that when I read them years from now, I will continue to find new meaning in them. The preceding dialogue is excerpted from our sixteenth session with the Team. This was our introduction to the Twelve Rays.

Overview of the Rays

The Twelve Rays can be divided into three separate groups: the Rays of Aspect, the Rays of Attributes, and the Rays of Soul Integration.

The first three Rays are referred to as the Rays of Aspect. They are the three aspects of the Creator that are filtered down through the various levels of creation before they enter into our dimension. They are filtered even further within our universe. Our physical bodies are not capable of receiving the full intensities of the Rays. The First Ray, the Ray of Divine Will, is filtered through the bear constellation known as Ursa Major. The Second Ray, the Ray of Love and Wisdom, is filtered through the triune star system Sirius, which is in the constellation known as Canis Major, the bigger dog. The Third Ray, the Ray of Active Intelligence, is filtered through the Pleiades. Each of these three areas acts as a focal point within our universe. They then direct the energy of the Rays to Earth.

The next group of Rays is known as the Rays of Attributes. They enable us to take on the multitude of human characteristics that provide us with the life experiences that are unique to this dimension. This group includes the Fourth Ray, the Ray Harmony through Conflict; the Fifth Ray, the Ray of Concrete Knowledge; the Sixth Ray, the Ray of Devotion and Idealism; and the Seventh Ray, which is known by a few names. The Team refers to the Seventh Ray as the Gateway into Awareness. I generally refer to it as the Violet Flame.

The Rays of Aspect and the Rays of Attributes comprise the first Seven Rays and have been written about and taught for hundreds of years. Alice Bailey wrote about the Rays extensively in her book *The Rays and the Initiations*, which was published in 1960. It is interesting to note that she only discusses the first Seven Rays in that publication.

The Rays of Soul Integration, Rays Eight through Twelve, have only become available within the last thirty years or so. Soul integration is a process now available to all of humankind. I will have much more to share about soul integration in the coming chapters. It is important to understand that Rays Eight through Twelve are the tools given to us to achieve soul integration.

The Team refers to the Eighth Ray as the Cleansing Ray, and it is used in conjunction with the Seventh Ray. The Ninth Ray, the Ray of Contact with the Soul Level, is used to connect with the higher aspects of self. The Tenth Ray is the Ray of the Body of Light and will be discussed extensively later. The Eleventh Ray is the Bridge to New Awareness. Before I discuss the New Awareness, let me point out that the Twelfth Ray is the New Awareness. I can't give you a definition of what the New Awareness is. I believe it is different for each individual. My hope is that by the end of this book, you will be able to tell me what your New Awareness is.

Each Ray represents a certain energetic frequency. This frequency is also symbolized by a color or a color pattern. Some Rays are a single color, while others are a blend of colors since they are a blend of Rays. The color of the individual Rays will be given as each Ray is introduced.

Julie and I were introduced to the Rays one Ray at a time. My sense of why it was done that way is that it gave us time to process and incorporate the frequency of each individual Ray separately. My recommendation is that, as you read about the Rays, you allow time in between each one to work with the exercises that are given. This will allow you to integrate each Ray into your physical structure.

We are taking you on a journey that involves permanently raising your energetic level as you go. There is no shortcut available. You will not be able to work with the higher Rays if you have not properly integrated the lower Rays into your energetic field. If at any time during your journey you find that the next Ray is for some reason blocked or you are not able to access it, ask yourself if you have really taken the time to integrate the preceding Ray's energies. It is a simple task to go back and repeat a step or two.

It is up to you to do the work. We hope that you have had experience with meditation in the past. If not, don't worry. You can go to our website and access free, guided meditations that will help you to become familiar with this very empowering self-practice. All the guided meditations presented in this book are also available on our website.

The answers that you are looking for are inside you. The path to the inner dimensions is inside you. The support that you need to accomplish whatever it is that you choose to achieve is accessible within you. Journeying inside, since at one time or another it is new to all of us, can be a daunting endeavor. Going where you have never gone before is often a challenge. We all enjoy maintaining the status quo. But there is something that compels us to move forward, to start the journey down a new road. You will be rewarded for your effort.

"You knew, and you still know, that you are on a greater journey to realize your divine equality with the Source itself, making you truly unlimited. Certainly free will on every level was given to you. But secondly, you were given the whole cocreator process within which to evolve your understanding. You step into that gradually as you become more and more aware of what it really means."

Our Divine Heritage

"You might say the First Ray energy says, 'This is new; let's get it done.' And the Second Ray energy says, 'Do it with love, and make sure the experience is true to yourself, your higher spirit.' And the Third Ray says, 'We must do this, and we must do this, and it must be done in this way,' and that gets it done. It focuses on the practical, and you find individual entities with a lot of this energy tend to be stubborn and driven and focused on the outcome."

CHAPTER 4

The Rays of Aspect

The first three Rays are referred to as the Rays of Aspect. They originate from the Source. Is this the only energy that emanates from the Source? I doubt it. These Rays are directed toward our universe and then further focused as they are stepped down toward our planet. It is interesting to note that all life forms benefit from the Rays. The Earth herself, for example, absorbs all the Rays.

When I think about the first three Rays, Divine Will, Love and Wisdom, and Active Intelligence, I can't help but be reminded of the Holy Trinity I learned about as a young Catholic school student: God existing simultaneously as the Father, the Son, and the Holy Spirit. Back then, I was taught that "divine will" meant God had a plan for each and every one of us, and He had given us His commandments to live by. Every time we disobeyed His commandments or weren't following His will, we got ourselves into trouble. I now understand Divine Will to mean that the Creator has given us the ability to also create. The Creator more or less got the ball rolling and then empowered us, its creations, to continue the process. I like to say that the Creator's creations continue creating. This feels very empowering to me.

If you think of an acorn that falls from a mighty oak tree, it has all of the traits that the oak tree has. As you examine the acorn it is hard to find those traits, but we all know they are there. I believe the same holds true for us in this dimension. I know it is very hard to imagine that we are imbued with the same traits the Creator has. I mean just take a look around. But those traits are indeed inside us, and we do quite legitimately have the potential to create heaven on Earth. The key is being able to see the divinity in yourself first and then in everyone else.

Love and wisdom are certainly aspects of Jesus. The Gospels in the New Testament are filled with the wisdom of Jesus as related through His parables. Without a shadow of doubt, love was what He talked about most. Jesus practiced love in everything He did. His legacy is one of love and wisdom. I think too many people focus on other events in His life and often forget about His teachings.

Active Intelligence is an interesting concept, and I will go into it in depth in just a bit. Going back to my Catholic roots again, the Holy Ghost, according to the Baltimore Catechism, "sanctifies souls through the gift of grace." Without getting too deep into a discussion of grace, it certainly is there to help us do good deeds. This is my understanding of Active Intelligence. It helps us to achieve what we wish to create. The assumption is that more often than not we desire to create things that help us and those around us.

A quick comment about the Merkaba that is referred to in the next chapter—I'll have more to say about it later. If you are not familiar with the Merkaba think of the six-sided Star of David. We most often only see the Star of David in pictures or print, and as such it is represented in two dimensions. When we add the third dimension, depth, we add two more points to each triangle, making each triangle a pyramid. The Merkaba then looks like two pyramids that have merged together. If you are having a difficult time envisioning this shape, then skip ahead to page 60 to see a picture. The Merkaba is often referred to as sacred geometry and has some specialized purposes—more on those a little bit later.

The follow chapter presents the first of our sessions with the team on the Rays. I've provided the dates of some of these sessions to give you an understanding of the timing of these sessions. Our very first recorded session was March 10, 2005. The following session was our twenty-first session. Here is the first mention by the team of the First Ray. The first sentence is me beginning the session.

CHAPTER 5

The First Ray

And now, if you will, please invite our team in on this November 8, 2005.

We sit with you, and we call forth a beautiful red energy to fill this Merkaba, to fill this space as you reside in this beauty of this energy. This is the energy of the First Ray, Divine Will, directed down through the layers of creation into your solar system through the many levels of your being. It is an energy of change, of allowing.

Whereas you invoke the First Ray, you step from that point of sameness onto the path of evolution and change. Divine Will is a characteristic of a higher consciousness, the drive and determination beyond the ego, it is a characteristic of the warrior, of which you are, and you will find it helpful when great change has taken place. It comes to you through your soul, stepping down into your personality, into your atomic structure, and helps bring greater awareness and vision to the larger picture.

Use this Ray and envision a ladder of pure red energy and use this energy when you feel stuck by apathy, by pain, by lack of vision, to help you climb through those lesser emotions. Climb this ladder one rung at a time, until you see the greater picture. We see the frustration; we see the unbinding. You feel unraveled, unstable, and it is these feelings that allow the new to come in. They make way for the changes.

It is no coincidence, I assume, that the First Ray, the red Ray, is given to us at the time when we can utilize it the most and experience it ourselves.

The First Ray comes through at times of great change. Your Earth is at a time of crisis and your soul also at a crossroads, both utilizing this first, most powerful Ray. And as you use this power to bring greater vision into your lives, you also bring greater vision to your planet.

I feel myself being filled with energy right now. More energy right now. I feel that we are remembering the use of the Merkaba, the power of the Merkaba.

Fill this space, this most holy spot with the light of this most holy energy and let it permeate each of your cells. Breathe it in, and as you do so, fill yourself with the wisdom that you know from your higher self, your spirit, the wisdom that you have remembered. And see your path. Vision your destination and see the light of the energy of those along your path. As you vision each of those energies, see the light grow brighter in yourself and the light along the path. So as you turn around and see where you have been, you see yourself as brighter. And as you turn again and look to the future of where you are to go, you see an even brighter light. This is your energy growing and expanding, and as you move, you pull with you those that desire to expand, those that you touch along your way.

This is a beautiful vision. Thank you.

Call on this energy, this Divine Will, whenever you are feeling less than the light that you are, whenever you feel paralyzed to choose the direction you know in your heart points you to the light—the greater, more expanded, brighter light.

Stop, Feel, and Listen

Before you read on and before you have had time to mentally process the information that you just read, take two minutes to do the following visualization exercise. They are not exercises given directly by the Team.

You'll have to trust me when I say that visualization is easy. We do it all the time. Just take a minute and think of a big, bright-yellow lemon. Now imagine taking a knife and slicing it in half. See how juicy it is. Now imagine cutting a nice big slice from one of the halves. Then cut that slice in half, and as you do, you can see the juice burst out of the lemon. Now pick it up and begin to move it toward your mouth. Move it closer and closer until you put it into your mouth and bite down on it. What did you taste? Did it cause any sensations in your mouth? Did you wince at all? OK, that was visualization.

Now read this next short paragraph and then put everything down and for two minutes visualize the image described.

See yourself seated with your hands resting gently in front of you on your lap. Feel your gentle, rhythmic breathing and allow the rich, red energy of the First Ray, the Ray of Divine Will, to gently and totally surround you. Just allow yourself to let go and feel the energy.

Take this time for yourself right now—just two minutes of your time to experience the energy of this Ray. You can do this two-minute exercise as many times as you choose. I would highly recommend that after each time you do this, you go back and read the information that the Team gave regarding the First Ray. I think you will find something new each time you repeat this quick exercise.

Now to really get value from this short exercise, in the space below write down any insights that may have occurred to you while you were processing this information.

 Discussion

The First Ray is called Divine Will. As I shared previously, I have a Catholic upbringing, and within that context when I hear the phrase Divine Will, I think of the Baltimore Catechism, certain portions of which we were required to memorize. Here's one that is still in my head. Question: what must we do to gain happiness of heaven? Answer: to gain happiness of heaven we must know, love, and serve God in this world. I find it amazing that it is still so clear in my mind.

My first understanding of Divine Will was God's desire for all of creation. Humankind was required to understand God's will and abide by it. It was often defined as mysterious, especially when we asked questions about how a loving God could have so much sorrow and pain as part of His plan. It seems to me that there is a bit of truth in many of our great religious dogmas. The part I agree with here is that there is a plan. I have trouble with the part that maintains it is all laid out and that we have to figure it out and abide by it.

I currently understand Divine Will as something different. I see God or the Source or All That Is as the Creator. And I believe that we have been created with the same attributes as the Creator. When you see the acorns on the ground underneath the mighty oak tree, you know that each has the potential to be a great oak in its own right. This is how I see our souls, as little creators at the feet of the Creator.

Here is a short comment from the Team about Divine Will.

Divine Will is an allowance, a gift to go and create, to design, to define this self that you recognize.

Divine Will then is that we learn how to use our talents and abilities. We learn how to create, and what we create helps to define who we are. That is exactly what we do every day of our lives. We create our own selves and our own realities. We constantly make choices that directly impact our experiences. The Creator's creations continue creating.

The squirrel carries the acorn off and buries it in the dirt where, if it is left alone, it will eventually sprout a root that anchors it and will send a sprout of leaves to break through the surface to tap the life-giving energies of the sun. We find ourselves here on Earth—not exactly carried here by squirrels, although there is that charming story of being carried by the storks—to use our abilities to create a life based on our choices. Through our lives, we continue the ongoing process of creation.

Let's begin the First Ray meditation. Whether you are new to meditation or are an experienced meditator, I'm sure you will find this meditation relaxing and insightful. Remember my suggestion for all the meditations in this book: read through each meditation completely before doing it. Then you can proceed using your memory alone. If this doesn't work very well for you, then let me suggest that you read the meditation into a recording device of some sort like your phone. Keep in mind that all of these meditations are also available to listen to free of charge on my web site at TheTwelveRays.com.

 First Ray Meditation: DIVINE WILL – PART ONE

Let's begin by taking a gentle, deep breath—gently inhaling and then slowly exhaling. You may close your eyes if you find that more relaxing. Please make sure your feet are firmly on the floor if you are sitting. Feel free to sit with your legs folded underneath you if that is more familiar to you. Now take another gentle, deep breath and again gently exhale.

Now I invite you to journey to your safe place. Journey to your sacred place, the place where you go to when you meditate, when you are alone. Travel there any way you choose. You may see yourself walking along a path to get there. You may feel yourself floating to get there, or you may simply find yourself there. Choose whatever way is best for you. And when you find yourself in that safe place, that sacred place, make yourself comfortable. You may choose to sit down in something comfortable, or perhaps you prefer to see yourself lying down, completely relaxed. Or maybe you would just rather stand. Do whatever you find to be the most comfortable.

When you are nice and comfortable, you may wish to call in your guides and teachers if you normally meditate with them. You might choose to call in your angels instead. If you don't normally connect with any other entities during your meditations it is fine to just be by yourself. That's right, nice and relaxed, feeling very comfortable.

Now I would like you to visualize a red light above your head. Allow this red light, this rich, vibrant light to represent the energy of the First Ray. Invite the First Ray to begin to penetrate your energetic field. Allow it to descend down toward the top of your head. Now allow the First Ray to begin to move through your body. Allow it to move past your head, surrounding you like a column of lush, vibrant red light. Allow it to continue to move down. See it now surrounding your abdomen. Allow it to move past your waist and down through your legs. Allow it to continue down into your feet and even further, flowing down into Mother Earth.

Now take the time to notice how you feel. What does this energy feel like? Do you feel it more strongly in any particular part of your body?

This is the energy of the First Ray, Divine Will, directed down through the layers of creation into our solar system through the many levels of your being. It is an energy of change, of allowing. When you invoke the First Ray, you step from that point of sameness onto the path of evolution and change. Divine Will is a characteristic of a higher consciousness, the drive and determination beyond the ego. It is a characteristic of the warrior, and you will find it helpful when great change has taken place. It comes to you through your soul, stepping down into your personality, into your atomic structure, and helps bring greater awareness and vision to the larger picture.

(Wait one minute.)

In a minute we will begin our journey back. Use this remaining time to communicate with your guides and teachers or any other entities who might have joined you today. Ask them if they have anything else to share with you today. Thank them for their continued help and guidance. Thank them for being here with you today.

(Wait one minute.)

When you are ready to return, begin your journey back by taking a gentle, deep breath. Slowly exhale and, as you do, begin to feel your fingers and your toes and begin to gently move them. As you begin to wiggle your fingers and your toes, allow your consciousness to begin to fully return to your physical body. As you feel your consciousness fully returning to your physical body, become aware of your arms and your legs. And when you are ready, gently open your eyes and return to this place and this time. Welcome back.

First Ray Meditation: DIVINE WILL – PART ONE
INSIGHTS

You will find the following worksheet really valuable to help put the experience you just had into a usable format. The time you spend in journaling your experience will pay off handsomely for you.

Insights: list as many as you can remember.

_____

_____

_____

Main concepts: what is the subject matter behind the concepts?

_____

_____

_____

Meaning for you: how do you interpret these insights?

_____

_____

_____

How can you use this in your daily life?

_____

_____

_____

Why is that helpful?

_____

_____

_____

Below is a second, shorter meditation that has a slightly different intention. It is an example of recent insights I have had after reflecting later on information from the Team. When we use our abilities to create, we sometimes find ourselves stuck. We may find ourselves procrastinating. I refer to this as resistance. We can use the First Ray to identify the source of the resistance. This is a very important aspect of being a creator. When resistance appears—and it will—we need to have a way to identify it and move beyond it. Here is what the Team says about resistance:

Call on this energy, this Divine Will, whenever you are feeling less than the light that you are, whenever you feel paralyzed to choose the direction you know in your heart points you to the light—the greater, more expanded, brighter light.

You can use the First Ray to identify the source of the resistance. Then work with the Third Ray to move beyond the resistance. I hope you enjoy this short meditation.

 First Ray Meditation: DIVINE WILL – PART TWO

Once again place your feet squarely on the floor or underneath you and take a gentle, relaxing, deep breath. You may wish to close your eyes to help you concentrate. Please make sure your feet are firmly on the floor if you are sitting. Feel free to sit with your legs folded underneath you if that is more familiar to you. Now take another gentle, deep breath and again gently exhale.

Now envision a ladder of pure red energy and focus on how you feel. Do you feel stuck by apathy, by pain, by lack of vision? Use this ladder to help you climb through those lesser emotions. Climb this ladder one rung at a time until you see the greater picture. Feel free to choose something other than a ladder to ascend if it makes you feel more comfortable. Perhaps a staircase would be more suitable?

Take a few minutes to allow that bigger picture to come into focus for you. You may need to climb just a little bit higher to move past those lesser emotions.

(Wait two minutes.)

Now with that bigger picture in view, what is the source of the resistance? What is holding you back? Remember that we are only looking to identify the source of the resistance. You will be able to understand how to move past this resistance when you work with the Third Ray. Focus now on getting the insights you need to identify the source of the resistance.

(Wait two minutes.)

In a minute, you will return to full waking consciousness. Before you do, I'd like you to remember that you can bring back with you the memory of all that you experienced in this First Ray meditation.

When you are ready to return to full waking consciousness, I'd like you to take a gentle, deep breath. Begin to wiggle your fingers and your toes. As you wiggle your fingers and your toes, feel your arms and your legs. And when you are ready, I'd like you to open your eyes and return to this place and this time. Welcome back.

Meditation is all about relaxing and using your imagination. If you didn't have the type of experience that you expected, don't get discouraged. Practice helps. Remember that there is no right or wrong way to meditate.

First Ray Meditation: DIVINE WILL – PART TWO
INSIGHTS

Insights: list as many as you can remember.

Main concepts: what is the subject matter behind the concepts?

Meaning for you: how do you interpret these insights?

How can you use this in your daily life?

Why is that helpful?

Summary and Key Concepts

- Divine Will is defined as All That Is bestowing on us the ability to create and manifest in this dimension and thereby continue the process of creation.
- We have a Divine Inheritance that is ours to claim. Embrace your heritage!
- The First Ray can be used to help identify resistance that we feel when we are ready to move forward, when we are ready to create something new.

Learnings

- Divine Will is a gift to go and create and define our selves.
- We create through our Divine Inheritance. The process that we use is beyond this dimension and is facilitated by the Twelve Rays.
- Thoughts are things. Everything that is manifested in this dimension started out as a thought first.
- We create our own realities with every thought we think and every choice we make.
- We all experience resistance in moving forward. It is a signal that something needs to be attended to.

CHAPTER 6

The Second Ray

The Second Ray, the Ray of Love and Wisdom, is a beautiful aqua-blue in color. Here is the first introduction of the Second Ray by the Team.

You have felt the Second Ray. It is the Ray of Love and Wisdom. On this Ray, the great spiritual leaders and teachers exist. This Ray is your doorway to the higher mental concepts that pass down from Source. As teachings from the spiritual hierarchy, concepts are placed in this universal mind. If you can allow yourself to stretch and open to these concepts, they are yours. This is why you may find that great teachings and concepts are attained by individuals throughout the whole of your world at the same time as they become available, and you have stretched to bring them into your reality. They can be made part of your soul through your spirit.

Using this Ray, you may bring in the pink light of love and dispel disharmony and bring clarity to your thought, to your surroundings, to your situation, by surrounding it in the aqua blue, the energy of wisdom.

We spend time with you on these Rays, the First, the Second, and the Third Ray that we will talk and you will experience more about, the Ray of Active Intelligence—these are Rays of Aspect. They affect you at all levels, for as you change through each thought, Source experiences change. As you use these Rays to perfect the value of the energies you hold, Source feels that perfection, and all that is between you and Source is never the same.

The Second Ray was given to us as a meditation in which we visualized our spiritual body infused with the blue-green energy, to form a cocoon around us. Is this the way we invoke the Second Ray?

Yes, bring in the colors and bring in the thought and the feeling of the moment, of the expression of those colors.

So when we bring in the pink energy of love as an aspect of the Second Ray, is it encapsulated by the Second Ray?

With your intention, with your conscious thought, so moves that energy.

 ## Stop, Feel, and Listen 🎵

Before you read on and before you have had time to mentally process the information that you just read, take two minutes to do the following exercise. Read this next sentence and then put everything down and for two minutes visualize the image described.

See yourself seated with your hands resting gently in front of you on your lap. Feel your gentle, rhythmic breathing and begin to wrap yourself in the luminous aqua-blue energy of the Second Ray, starting at your feet and working your way up to your head until you are totally surrounded in this loving energy.

Again, to really get value from this short exercise, write down any insights that may have occurred to you while you were processing this information.

I recommend that you go back now and read the information that the Team gave us on the Second Ray. Did you get any different meaning than the last time you read it? You may bring in the Second Ray as often as you choose. See what happens every time you reread the text after doing the visualization.

Here is some additional information that the Team provided about the Second Ray.

You ask many questions about the energy of the Rays, how to use them, when to use them. We have given you some instruction on their use. We tell you they all come from Source, originate. Together they are filtered through the universe, through the dimensions. They are stepped down.

Let us speak specifically of the Second Ray. It filters down through Sirius and from Sirius projected onto Earth. Why is this? Because the intent of that planet, the focus of energy on the planet, draws the Ray, attracts it. It is magnified, and it is projected through conscious intent from that pinpoint. Is this the only projection from this Ray, for this Ray? No. There are many galaxies, many dimensions. But your focus from your vantage point on Earth reaching out is aware of this energy emanating from this location because of its great magnitude. The other Rays are projected in a similar fashion, all available.

 Discussion

We use the Second Ray to connect to the Creator's love. Most of us have a very strong appreciation of human love. It is something we constantly strive to surround ourselves with. Divine Love is the source of all human love, but we seldom seek it. We seldom attempt to connect with it. It seems like an abstraction for many of us. And for others, there is sometimes a misguided belief that we don't deserve love of any sort. It is very rewarding not only to feel deserving of the Creator's love but also to know that it is there waiting for us to accept it. All we need to do is to open our hearts to it.

That may sound easy, but in actuality it may be very difficult to open our hearts to any form of love. Many of us have had unpleasant life experiences in the past that have led us to understand that experiencing human love can make us very vulnerable to heartbreak and pain. It is important to keep in mind that Divine Love never leads to pain or suffering. As a matter of fact, we would all do well to remember that when we do experience the ups and downs of human love, we can always reach out to Divine Love to help us deal with our emotions. Connecting with Divine Love then helps us to transcend the heartbreaks of human love.

The Second Ray also helps us to feel connected to something larger than our individual, personal perspectives. As the Team points out, the great spiritual leaders and teachers exist on this Ray. We use this Ray to help us tap into higher mental concepts. How do these higher concepts help? They provide a different perspective, and these alternative perspectives enable us to redefine our experiences. They help us to see things from a different angle. That new and different perspective just might bring a totally new understanding of our experiences that could lead to some positive personal changes. Make no mistake about it—life is full of changes. Life is full of growth opportunities. Many people expend sizable amounts of energy trying to inhibit change. Many struggle so hard to maintain the status quo. My suggestion to those individuals is to face facts. We are all experiencing change. Save your energy and learn how to enjoy change as opposed to struggling against it in vain.

When we use the Second Ray, we connect to Divine Love. We cannot experience the full intensity of Divine Love in this dimension. What we *can* experience is further reduced by our own energetic levels. As I mentioned earlier, one of the benefits of working with the Twelve Rays is that we have the opportunity to raise our own, individual energetic levels. As we raise our own energetic levels, we have not only the opportunity to experience the higher mental concepts that are available on the Second Ray, but also the potential to experience a higher expression of Divine Love.

The Second Ray is used in conjunction with the First Ray to guide us as creators. All that we see in this manifested universe is a result of the First Ray of creation combined with the Second Ray of Love and Wisdom. It reminds us to create from a place of love. We should always keep this in mind. When we follow the example of the Creator, when we create with love, the things that we manifest in this dimension will necessarily lead us to that which we came here to experience.

The Merkaba

The Second Ray meditation uses the Merkaba that I mentioned earlier. Let me provide some additional information about the Merkaba. It is an ancient symbol and part of what is often referred to as sacred geometry. Technically, it is described as a star tetrahedron. A tetrahedron is a four-sided triangle, like a pyramid. Each side has the exact same dimensions.

I'm sure many are familiar with the Star of David. That symbol is a two-dimensional representation of the Merkaba. The Merkaba is the union of two opposing tetrahedrons. As they come together, they merge in three-dimensional space and create the eight-pointed star. It is this coming together that is most important, for the Merkaba represents the synthesis of two opposing concepts.

Here is a discussion with the Team about the Merkaba and some mention of the duality of this dimension. We are again invited to create as we have never created before.

> *There is a separateness that each of you felt as you were birthed into this world, this dimension of duality. There is a saying you know, "As above so below." Not yet have we seen as below so above, yet the potential—the potential is there, for the spiritual, your spiritual essence, mirrors your physical divinity. We point out you have a symbol, the light and the dark, the yin and the yang, the male and the female, and it is only correct in its symbolism as it moves and spirals and mixes together, for it remains as a symbol of separateness.*
>
> *You hold the truth of the Merkaba within you, the mixing of the male and the female, the Earth and the sky. They spin each of them in two different directions. And they fuse, they mix, and in the center the movement is so fast there is no separation between one direction or the other. Stand in the center, in the stillness although not still and know at that point, at that very center point, all has combined. It is that duality that was created that allows each of you to become creators on this level, in this dimension knowing as you grow that you can move higher on the spiral. Join us. Create at a higher level. Move mountains.*

I asked a question about a particular form of Merkaba meditation, and I decided not to mention the name here. It really isn't about one form of meditation being better than another. They did, however, answer the question.

There are many meditations, some more popular than others. What we have asked and what you have agreed, long before you came to this life, is for you to take this time, and you understand this enough to say, do not limit yourself to one way. There are many helpful tools, but the time has come for you to know there is no one method, no one meditation that you must follow to activate, specifically talking about the Merkaba.

Just stand in the Merkaba, hold it in your thought—your grand thought within you—expand it, draw in the energies that you hold, the love in your heart, and ignite that Merkaba—that energy within it—through your intention. Manifest.

Our reality as we know it today is full of duality. We see light and dark as opposites just as we see hot and cold as opposites. The experience of duality goes on and on—male/female, old/young, poor/rich, and so forth. We even have the duality of spiritual and physical—that which doesn't have shape, form, and matter versus that which does, which includes just about anything you can perceive with your physical senses.

What is important about bringing together opposites? Take the example of hot and cold. Is cold good? How about hot? Is it good? The answer is it depends. Some people might say the cold in Alaska is not so good. An ice-cold beverage in Florida's noonday heat is a different story. Someone from Alaska might say the opposite. When we look at these extremes and then bring that information together, we form a synthesis. What we are really talking about here is temperature. Hot and cold merely represent the extremes of temperature. When we form a synthesis, we understand the true essence of the extremes. When we form a synthesis of male and female, we understand the wisdom, the essence of gender.

I use the Merkaba in three different ways, and each way involves the Second Ray. The first technique for the Merkaba is one I find most interesting. I use it to go back to sleep. I often wake up in the middle of the night, and my mind seems to be going a mile a minute. I simply create my personal Merkaba, and wham—I'm back sleeping. The second way I use the Merkaba is when I work one-on-one with clients. When I begin to work with a new client, I will often guide them in the creation of their own personal Merkaba. Another more traditional use of the Merkaba is as a portal to the inner dimensions. In all three instances, I create the Merkaba in the same way. This particular technique uses the two opposites of spiritual and material or physical to create the synthesis of the two.

Let's begin the Second Ray meditation. It is longer than the two meditations offered so far. Just read through this entire script once and get a feel for it. Because of the length of it, I strongly recommend that you record it into your phone or some other recording device and play it back. Alternatively, you can go to the website and hear the audio file that is already recorded there.

Second Ray Meditation: USING THE MERKABA

As we begin this meditation for the Second Ray, I'd like you to get comfortable in your chair. If you have anything on your lap, please put it on the floor now. Just gently relax your hands either in your lap or at your sides. Have your feet resting comfortably beneath you, either on the floor or folded in some way. Take a relaxing, deep breath, and as you exhale, breathe out any stress or anxiety that you may be feeling. Continue to focus on your breath and maintain a gentle, rhythmic breathing pattern. Good.

Now I'd like you to bring your awareness to your crown chakra at the top of your head. I'd like you to visualize the beautiful violet energy of the Creator. This energy is always with you. Now invite that energy, that beautiful violet energy to move into your body. Invite it to move down through your brow chakra, also called the third-eye chakra. Allow it to keep moving down to your throat chakra. Now allow it to continue to move down until it comes to rest in your heart center. And when it reaches your heart center, we want to give this energy intention. For today, we give this energy our intention of love and healing, kindness, compassion, forgiveness, higher self-realization, and gratitude.

Now I'd like you to bring your awareness to your root chakra at the base of your spine. Envision the beautiful red energy of Mother Earth. This energy is also constantly with you. Invite this energy to begin to rise up into your body. Allow it to rise into your sacral chakra, which is located just below your navel. Allow it to continue to rise through your abdomen until it reaches your solar plexus just below your heart center. Allow it to continue to rise until it now reaches your heart center. And when it has reached your heart center, we again want to give this energy intention. Again for today, we give this energy our intention of love and healing, connection with Mother Earth, loving relationships, higher self-esteem, abundance in all things, and gratitude.

Now bring these two energies together, bringing the two pyramids together, and as you do, allow them to expand creating your personal Merkaba. Allow this Merkaba to expand so much that it totally surrounds you. Feel yourself totally encompassed by your Merkaba.

And now we set the pyramids into motion by spinning them in opposite directions. The top pyramid, which is pointing downward, represents the energy of the Creator and spins in a counterclockwise direction. The bottom pyramid, which is pointing upwards, represents the energy of Mother Earth and spins in a clockwise direction. Allow them to spin so fast that you no longer can really tell that they are spinning at all.

See yourself standing in the middle of this beautiful Merkaba. Bring in the energy of the Second Ray. Bring in the luminescent, aqua-blue energy of the Second Ray and begin to wrap it around you. Start from your feet and wrap it around just like you were wrapping up an Egyptian mummy. Continue to wrap this energy around you until it forms an energetic cocoon all around you. And when you have completed wrapping yourself, take a moment and feel yourself surrounded by this beautiful, luminescent, aqua-blue energy of the Second Ray.

And now envision the pink energy of the Second Ray. This is the aspect of love contained in this Ray. Move this energy around your heart. Envision your heart to be surrounded by this beautiful, pink energy of love. Take a moment and think about how you have protected your heart based upon your past experiences, your past hurts. Think about the defense that you have established to protect your heart. Now feel this pink energy begin to penetrate those defenses and feel them begin to soften. We don't want to dismantle any of these defense mechanisms just now. We just want to feel them beginning to soften as this pink energy of love penetrates them.

Now connect to your heart, the physical organ in your chest. Ask it how it feels to be surrounded by this pink energy of love. Ask it if it is ready to open to a higher expression of love. Ask it if it is willing to work with you to allow this higher expression of love, this energy of the Second Ray, to be a part of your experience going forward. And as you contemplate opening your heart to this higher expression of love, know that before you can really offer love to anyone else, you must first offer it to yourself. You must first be willing to forgive yourself and accept self-love. And once you have opened your heart to self-love, you may then experience this higher love in your relationships with others. But before you can truly love others, you must first love yourself.

You are capable of opening fully to the love that is within your heart. Again, feel your heart surrounded by this beautiful, pink energy of the Second Ray, the energy of love. Feel it once again as it begins to soften all of those defenses that have been put in place to protect it. Know that you go at your own pace as you soften those defenses, never going any faster than you choose to. You are in complete control. Feel how good that feels.

In a minute we will begin to bring your awareness back to your physical body. Take this time to thank your heart for all the love that it holds for you. Thank it for all the ways that it has supported you so far in your journey. And thank it for its willingness to move forward with you as you open to this higher expression of love that the Second Ray reminds you of.

Now once again focus your awareness on your breathing. Take a gentle, deep breath, and as you do, begin to allow your consciousness to return to your physical body. Continue with your rhythmic breathing. Gently begin to wiggle your fingers and your toes, and as you do, once again feel the connection with your arms and your legs. Continue to allow your consciousness to return to your body, and when you are ready, gently open your eyes and return to this place and this time, fully relaxed and feeling calm and peaceful. Welcome back.

Second Ray Meditation: USING THE MERKABA
INSIGHTS

Insights: list as many as you can remember.

Main concepts: what is the subject matter behind the concepts?

Meaning for you: how do you interpret these insights?

How can you use this in your daily life?

Why is that helpful?

I know each meditation experience is unique, and I know that everyone will more or less evaluate their experience to determine whether they were successful in their own minds. I try to help people understand that there is no right or wrong way to meditate. Everyone has a unique ability to go within, and some have had more practice with it than others. Experience does make a difference. Rest assured that if you didn't have the experience you were anticipating, you should not consider it a failure. There is plenty of information in each and every meditation, and very often clues are provided that will enable you to progress further the next time.

Summary and Key Concepts

- The Second Ray is the source of Divine Love in this dimension.
- The higher mental concepts that pass down from the Source are communicated to humankind through this Ray.
- When we create, we should make sure that we always do it out of love.
- The Merkaba is a star tetrahedron and is part of what is called sacred geometry. It can be used to represent the union or synthesis of opposites.

Learnings

- Human love is derived from the source of all love, which is Divine Love.
- The belief that anyone is not worthy of love is an illusion.
- We can increase our experience of Divine Love and human love by raising our individual energetic levels. This is one of the benefits of working with the Twelve Rays.
- When we create out of love, we are being true to our real selves.
- The Merkaba and other components of sacred geometry are available for us to use.
- I use the Merkaba to help me to fall asleep.

CHAPTER 7

The Third Ray

The Third Ray completes the group of Rays known as the Rays of Aspect. It seems to me a critical element, and it is key to manifesting in this dimension.

The Third Ray that you are actively experiencing is called the Ray of Active Intelligence. This Third Ray is used to get the job done. It is a Ray of organization. Most healers are filled with a lot of this Ray energy, and as it is used to organize, sometimes awareness is not given to the consequences. From this Ray—this Third Ray—flow the Fourth, the Fifth, the Sixth, and the Seventh. They flow through this Third Ray allowing the organization and the process to manifest and create.

You might say the First Ray energy says, "This is new; let's get it done." And the Second Ray energy says, "Do it with love, and make sure the experience is true to yourself, your higher spirit." And the Third Ray says, "We must do this, and we must do this, and it must be done in this way," and that gets it done. It focuses on the practical, and you find individual entities with a lot of this energy tend to be stubborn and driven and focused on the outcome.

Stop, Feel, and Listen

Before you read on and before you have had time to mentally process the information that you just read, take two minutes to do the following exercise. Read this next sentence then put everything down and for two minutes visualize the image described.

See yourself seated with your hands resting gently in front of you on your lap. Feel your gentle, rhythmic breathing and visualize a column of golden-yellow light descending upon you from above. Allow this energy to move through you. This is the Ray that shows you how to manifest that which you desire to experience.

One more time, write down below any insights that may have occurred to you while you were processing this information.

Now that you have felt the energy of the Third Ray, you know that whenever you wish to manifest something in your life, you can use this Ray to help you to understand the steps needed to complete the task.

There is another aspect of the Third Ray that I would like to share with you. Here is a brief exchange between the Team and me:

> *Utilize the Third Ray to focus—to focus on your goals, to place your intention. It will help to set into motion, to light the path. It will light the way towards you, but hold your intention clear, visualize, and be clear on what you intend to draw, what you wish to see, both for yourself and your planet.*

> So the Third Ray corresponds to what we have often referred to as the Law of Attraction?

> *It can be defined that way. It is an expansive energy.*

I found it surprising that the Team would also point out that the Third Ray could be used to bring what you wish to manifest towards you. As you can see, I immediately thought of the Law of Attraction, and they confirmed that the Third Ray is the energy behind the Law. I find it always helps to understand more fully how things operate.

The Team also provided an insight into using the Third Ray to manifest our desires. This message was delivered outside of the discussion of the Third Ray. However, it seems to be a clear description of the process of personal manifestation.

> *We'd also like to repeat a message given to you much earlier in our discussions. We cannot emphasize enough the importance of learning to*

focus your attention, to consciously focus the energy of your thought and feelings and directing that energy through love. When you learn to do this, when you remember, it will speed the process of manifestation. You will create instantaneously that which you desire.

 Discussion

The Third Ray is the Ray of Active Intelligence. I like to refer to it as the "get 'er done Ray." This Ray provides insights as to how you bring whatever you choose to create to fruition. It will help you understand the individual steps you need to take to get it done. In my mind, this is a different process than the Law of Attraction. Here is how I think it differs.

We use the Third Ray to get clarity on what it takes to get something done. We may set a goal for ourselves—let's say you want to start a vegetable garden. You may not know the first thing about growing vegetables or gardening. So you sit down, quiet yourself, bring in the Third Ray, and just be open to what steps you need to do and in what sequence in order to be successful with your new garden.

Perhaps the first idea that pops into your mind is to get a book on gardening and read it. Then the next idea that comes is you should start composting your kitchen scraps. Then you think that taking a class from your local gardening society would introduce you to the particular characteristics of the area that you live in, like what plants do best and how long the growing season is. After you get about a dozen of these ideas into your head, you then start ordering them into a sequence. This is what I do first; this is what I do second; this comes next; then this.

This is what we primarily use the Third Ray for. It helps us to see what needs to be done, and then it helps us to create the sequence in which to do them. This is how you get 'er done! How many times have you started a project without much preparation and at the end discovered that either you left a few things out of your planning or you did things in a less than effective sequence?

Once the goal has been decided on and the plan is in place, then you can use the Third Ray's Law of Attraction aspect to draw resources you need to you. I don't intend to say here that there is only one way to work with the Law of Attraction. I believe this approach is just one of the ways to work with the Law. If you have a process that is different, and it works for you, then by all means stick to what you know works. If, however, you are open to trying something different, then see how this approach works for you. The Third Ray meditation that follows will take you through the steps for using this approach.

The last quote from the Team is particularly important. They mentioned this more than once during our sessions. I think it supports the concept that thoughts are things. It also emphasizes the concept that our attention is what leads to manifestation in this dimension. That is why they put so much emphasis on learning to focus our attention and holding that focus. Don't be confused by their stating that we will learn to create instantly. Before anything can be manifested, it must be first created as a concept or an idea or a thought. Then through our focused attention, it becomes manifested over time in this dimension.

If you are ready to give this a try, then jump into the next meditation. Remember to keep these two concepts separate. The first concept is what does it take to manifest something (the plan), and the second concept is actually manifesting it (drawing the resources to you to get it done).

 Third Ray Meditation: GET 'ER DONE

As we begin this meditation for the Third Ray, the Ray of Active Intelligence, I suggest that you get comfortable in your chair or some other place where you can sit relaxed. Gently relax your hands either in your lap or at your sides. Have your feet resting comfortably beneath you, either on the floor or folded in some way. You may start with your eyes either open or gently closed. Now take a relaxing, deep breath, and as you exhale, breathe out any stress or anxiety that you may be feeling. Continue to focus on your breath and maintain a gentle, rhythmic breathing pattern. Good.

Use this Third Ray to manifest anything you choose to bring into your reality. Once you get a clear idea of what it is you wish to create, the next step is to focus your attention on the goal and use your imagination to see it already manifested. When you feel it already manifested, then connect with that feeling of it now being part of your reality. How does it feel to now have that as part of your experience in this dimension? And as you continue to hold that connection to your already manifested goal, allow the action steps required to make it real in this dimension to enter into your consciousness.

Let's begin using this golden-yellow energy, the energy of the Ray of Active Intelligence. See yourself in your sacred place, the place you go to feel your connection with your whole self. And as you feel that connection grow stronger, you remember your abilities as a cocreator of this reality. You remember the way you manifest anything you choose in the higher dimensions. Now direct the energy of the Third Ray, this golden-yellow energy to flow through you. See it flowing around and through you any way you choose.

Remember that the first step in working with the Ray of Active Intelligence is to have a clear understanding of what you wish to manifest. If you desire happiness, what in particular would that experience of happiness look like? How would you know that you were experiencing happiness? If your goal is to manifest abundance, what would be a concrete manifestation of that abundance? How would you know that you had achieved your intended abundance? Take a minute now and get that clear image of what you wish to manifest. Define it as clearly as possible and then establish how you will know that it has indeed been created. Take a couple of minutes now to complete this first step.

(Wait one minute.)

Now let's move on to step two. See your goal as complete. Envision the end result. Verify that the conditions you need to convince yourself that you have indeed completed your objective have been met. Allow yourself to feel what it's like to have this manifested goal as part of your reality. Really feel it. Is it what you thought it would feel like, or is it perhaps more than even you had imagined? Allow that feeling of your completed objective to be absolutely real for you. How does it feel?

(Wait one minute.)

Now while you feel the satisfaction of your completed goal, allow the steps necessary to bring it into this dimension to enter your awareness. Allow the plan to bring your goal into your physical reality to fully develop—or at least develop to the point that you know what to do next to accomplish your goal. You may not receive all the steps that are required right now. There may be choices you will have to make along the way, and depending on the choices you make, you may have a variety of possible steps to take. All those steps may not show up today, and that is fine. Just make sure you have enough to begin the process. Take a minute or two now to allow the plan to come into your awareness.

(Wait one minute.)

In a minute we will begin to bring your awareness back to your physical body. Before we do though, if there is any detail you feel you have not received, take a moment and ask how this will be communicated to you in the future and listen for a response.

(Wait ten seconds.)

When you have everything you need to create your desired goal in this dimension, send your appreciation to your whole self for supporting you in this journey, in this lifetime. Acknowledge the constant support that you receive that makes your experience here in this dimension possible. Remember that you are a constant projection of your whole self.

Now once again focus your awareness on your breathing. Take a gentle, deep breath, and as you do, begin to allow your consciousness to return to your physical body. Continue with your rhythmic breathing. Gently begin to wiggle your fingers and your toes, and as you do, once again feel the connection with your arms and your legs. Continue to allow your consciousness to return to your body, and when you are ready, gently open your eyes and return to this place and this time, fully relaxed and feeling calm and peaceful. Welcome back.

Third Ray Meditation: GET 'ER DONE
INSIGHTS

Insights: list as many as you can remember.

_____

_____

_____

_____

Main concepts: what is the subject matter behind the concepts?

_____

_____

_____

_____

Meaning for you: how do you interpret these insights?

_____

_____

_____

_____

How can you use this in your daily life?

_____

_____

_____

_____

Why is that helpful?

_____

_____

_____

_____

The first three Rays—Divine Will, Love and Wisdom, and Active Intelligence—all come directly from the Source and together create all the higher Rays. Rays Four through Seven are created from the Third Ray, and the remaining Rays, Eight through Twelve, are combinations of the previous seven Rays.

I hope you have had the opportunity to work with the Rays of Aspect. Perhaps you would like to share your experiences with the rest of us. You can do that by going to our website and blogging your story. I highly encourage you to take the time to share.

Before we finish our discussion of the Rays of Aspect, I would like to share with you an additional comment from the Team.

> *What you are experiencing—what you have experienced through each exercise that we have given you—is a glimpse of the use for each of these main three Rays, to incorporate them to create that which serves you. As you evolve and change, you find yourselves in a time of turmoil, a time of decision. And it is a dangerous time for the human entity, for it is a time to examine what are you, what do you want to be, which parts of yourself do not work for you. What is your goal, knowing goals change in this moment? What is your goal? What parts of you, your personality, your limits, must you let go of to move forward, to achieve, to get it done—what you know in your heart is your desire to achieve?*
>
> *So this time is a time of choice, of letting go, for each of you. What do you choose to let go of, and what do you replace it with? We are here to offer you guidance and insight, yet you have choice. You can choose to integrate the knowledge you have been given or choose to walk away.*

You no doubt gather from the above text that each and every one of us has choice. This is a theme that the Team has consistently emphasized to us. They have never suggested one course of action as right or more desirable over another. There is no judgment on their part. They have supported us no matter what choices we have made, and some of our choices have taken us in the wrong direction, but that is my judgment and not theirs. Your level of desire to work with the information and exercises that have been given so far is totally up to you to decide. You can choose to jump in with both feet, or you may perhaps just skip over this section. The choice is entirely up to you. Remember that no matter what choice you make now, you can always choose differently later.

Summary and Key Concepts

- The Third Ray is used to get the job done. I call it the get 'er done Ray.
- From this Ray flow the Fourth, Fifth, Sixth, and Seventh Rays.
- The Third Ray provides the steps needed to manifest your desires, and it even provides the sequence in which to do them.
- The Law of Attraction is part of the Third Ray.

Learnings

- You create your own reality.
- It is highly beneficial to learn how to focus your attention. This is the key to manifestation in this dimension.
- You have created both the good and the bad in your life.
- When you take responsibility for your thoughts, you will think differently.
- Your imagination is one of your most important gifts. Use it often, and you will be rewarded.

Human Experiences

"Each individual has a little bit of each of these Rays. Some, depending on their talents and personalities, draw through them more of one than the other."

CHAPTER 8

The Rays of Attributes

We all have various personality attributes that make us individuals. This creates a beautiful tapestry of personality traits that make each and every one of us unique. These attributes have been thoughtfully combined to provide the resources we need for our individual journeys in this dimension.

It is easy to hold judgment about our individual attributes. Why am I this way, or why can't I be more like her or him? My sister got all the good looks in the family, while I did well in school. I'm just a plain Jane. It's not fair. My brother is a natural-born athlete. He was good at any sport he played. My little sister is a rebel. She is the artist. Mom and Dad let her get away with everything. My brother Joey is a born salesman. He can sell ice to Eskimos. The judgments go on and on.

It is easy to judge when we forget what our souls' plans are. We come to this dimension with intention. We are not just dropped off at a summer camp—"See you in two weeks. Have fun." A great deal of planning goes into each and every incarnation. Human personality traits are a very important part of that planning, and as we will soon see, the Rays of Attributes help reinforce those individual character traits. Here is the first introduction to the Rays of Attributes from the Team.

> *We last spoke of the Third Ray, the Ray of Active Intelligence. Through this Ray, Earth's lessons are learned, and the Creator experiences through the cosmic plan. Through this Ray, traveling through from Source to your planet, flow the Fourth, the Fifth, the Sixth, and the Seventh Rays.*
>
> *Rays Four through, particularly through, Six—let us exclude Ray Seven for a moment—these are Rays of Attributes. Each of you accesses varying amounts of the energies in these Rays depending on what you*

are experiencing, your personality, your mission, the plan, when you were called upon. Fear not in using them, but use them in their highest potential, in the clearest, highest vibration of each. Use them delicately. Use them with the wisdom, the love, the intelligence, and the will provided through the first three Rays.

Each individual has a little bit of each of these Rays. Some, depending on their talents and personalities, draw through them more of one than the other.

CHAPTER 9

The Fourth Ray

The Fourth Ray—the Fourth Ray can be called Harmony through Conflict, and most that experience this Ray first experience the conflict. Then through raising up the vibration, they can move into harmony. We associate a vibrational color of green to this Ray energy. And you find that most artists and musicians hold a great deal of this energy. They experience both outer and inner conflict. They wrestle with this as they create and struggle to find that harmonious place.

Energies of this Fourth Ray tend to affect people in very emotional ways, and individuals that are experiencing this Ray tend to be very earthbound in their activities. They enjoy activities such as hiking, mountain climbing, horseback riding, working in the dirt, being with Mother Nature. And they tend to find, when in a situation of conflict, that they spin around and around, and then other emotions tend to go high and low much like a roller coaster.

They tend to live and focus a great amount of energy in their solar plexus, which is a very emotional chakra. And to balance them, they need to travel; they need to raise their energies higher, into the mind. This is a natural balance, to lift their energy from the solar plexus region. And they need to work on moving this energy on the Fourth Ray to a higher vibration and find this harmonious state.

When you mentioned the Fourth Ray—the conflict and the harmony—conflict can only happen—it seems to me—where there is duality, and the physical plane is defined by many as being the reality of duality. Isn't that why people come here to learn through conflict? And is there a way to avoid that?

There is no way to avoid conflict as a human in your environment unless you place yourself in a comatose state. If you were to go and sit on a mountain, you could not escape conflict, for your mind would begin to wander to the valley below. You have senses in your physical body. You have senses in your spiritual body. You are here in this environment of perfect duality to have that opportunity to live, to feel, to exercise each one of your senses in the manner that you so choose. Some individuals thrive on conflict.

And they very rarely feel the harmony.

It is not their goal. Perhaps that is what they choose coming into their life. Perhaps they chose an extreme. Most choose to exist somewhere in between, and they do just that, exist somewhere in between. For others, there is more purpose served to move into a more harmonious vibration. Their job, as they see it, is showing others the possibilities, of giving others hope, showing others that higher extreme.

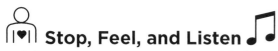 Stop, Feel, and Listen

It is time to once again to stop and feel. Read the following visualization and take two minutes to sit in the energy of the Fourth Ray. Allow yourself to relax and get quiet and then visualize.

Visualize a beautiful, peaceful, safe place where you can go in your mind. Let all the concerns and thoughts of your current experience, your current day, be on hold for the next two minutes. See yourself seated in a comfortable position. Take a deep relaxing breath and breathe out any tension or stress that you may be feeling. Invite your special friends to be with you. Envision or sense the energy of the Fourth Ray as a vibrant green. Direct this energy to come to you. You may feel it within you, perhaps in the third chakra. You may see it as a column of light descending from above. Or you may see it as a pool of pure energy that you walk into and be immersed in. Choose the most appropriate way for you to connect with it now and allow yourself to deeply feel the wisdom of this Ray.

I suggest that you write down below any insights that may have occurred to you while you were processing this information.

Remember that there is no escaping conflict. It is an integral part of this dimension. We, however, choose how to experience the conflicts. We can stay chained to them and expend our energies moving from one to the next until we find ourselves exhausted. Or we can understand that each and every conflict is an opportunity to experience the duality that exists so exquisitely here. And when we have fully grasped the significance of the experience, the essence of it, we can transform it and experience the harmony.

 Discussion

The Fourth Ray is called Harmony through Conflict. If we take a look at the history of our world for the past couple thousand years, we can certainly trace the ongoing conflict that has been our heritage.

Our earliest conflicts were with our gods. The Hebrews disobeyed their god and lost paradise because of it. Other early civilizations interpreted the events of Mother Nature as being directed by the gods. When the weather was bad, the gods were angry. It seems every culture creates its own mythology about its gods and then strives to stay on good terms with them. But eventually something happens, and there is a price to pay in order to regain their good graces.

When we weren't clashing with our gods, we always had the neighbors to fight with. Humankind has never stopped waging war against itself, and things don't seem to be getting any better. In fact, the twentieth century, which many deem the bloodiest century ever, witnessed the death of over 240 million people through war and other man-made causes. The twenty-first century isn't getting off to such a good start. There are wars all over the globe—some bigger and some smaller. I think it is safe to say that on the whole, there has been more conflict in our history than harmony.

We can also look at conflict on a personal level. Most of us have to provide for our families and ourselves. Providing food, safety, and shelter for our loved ones and ourselves is a top priority. We abide by laws in civilized societies that help to minimize our daily conflicts, but there are still such influences as work-related stress, relationship issues, and emotional issues that influence our mental and physical well-being and contribute to all kinds of personal conflicts.

You might wonder where all the harmony is. Sometimes it is difficult to find. We come here to experience life. We choose particular experiences for each visit. Sometimes we are men; sometimes we are women. Sometimes we are wealthy; sometimes we are poor. Sometimes we are law abiding; sometimes we are scoundrels. And when we have had enough experience seeing both sides, we can experience the middle. We can create a synthesis that incorporates both extremes. You may think there is no middle for gender, but think about it for a while. How would you refer to the gay and lesbian community?

After an individual has gained enough experience through conflict, harmony ensues. When you have had enough experience being both wealthy and poor, you understand that money doesn't buy happiness. You understand that poor people as well as rich people can lead healthy, happy, and loving lives. Breaking laws may seem to be glamorous for some, but most will understand the peace that abiding by the law brings. It goes on and on. Gaining experience can seem quite disruptive, but when duality has been experienced, then harmony can be established. Since this most often occurs at a personal level, it is often hard to see progress on a larger scale.

The Fourth Ray is very useful in dealing with emotional issues. As the team pointed out, artists and musicians tend to have a lot of this Ray. I believe the Team is also referring to all artistic expressions. I immediately think of writers and actors and dancers, but how about athletes, teachers, chefs, or anyone else who strives for personal expression? All of us who are involved in developing new techniques for personal expression can benefit from working with this energy.

It has long been held that spiritual growth requires pain and suffering. We are taught as small children that when we make sacrifices, we will at some point be rewarded. Some live their entire lives in pain and suffering believing that they will be rewarded for it.

It doesn't have to be this way going forward. We are moving into an era when spiritual growth through grace and ease will replace the pain and suffering model. We need not suffer any longer. Before each one of us can move into this new paradigm, however, we must rid ourselves of the lower-level energy that has accumulated through pain and suffering. Unfortunately, most of us need to operate within the context of the old paradigm to release and transmute that lower-level energy. I could tell you that you can release it through the new paradigm of grace and ease, but you probably wouldn't believe me since you created it using the old paradigm. I probably wouldn't believe me either.

So we find ourselves more or less in this interim period with one foot in the past and one foot in the future. Most of us need to use the old paradigm to move forward. So we can continue to use this Fourth Ray to help us understand the true nature of this reality, and by finding the synthesis within the duality, we can resolve the conflict and move forward. I hope that makes sense.

This notion of using the same tools that created the problem to resolve the problem has more to do with our limited beliefs of our own abilities than anything else. At the same time, we really are in this transition period when only some of the new ways of experiencing spiritual growth makes sense to us. We must be willing to put behind us what we have been used to in the past. What we are really talking about here is the nature of change and just how rapidly it takes place. For most, it is a process that takes time. So the need to continue to use the Fourth Ray isn't going to disappear anytime soon.

 Fourth Ray Meditation: CREATING HARMONY

The Fourth Ray, the Ray of Harmony through Conflict, has a vibrational color of green. We are told that artists and musicians tend to have a great deal of this energy. They tend to experience both inner and outer conflict and wrestle with this as they create and struggle to find that harmonious place. I believe that all artists use this energy in the process of creation. When I use the term "artist," I extend it to all types of performers, dancers, actors, magicians, and so on. I also extend the term to anyone perfecting a skill. I consider woodcrafters, writers, poets, athletes, and so on to be artists.

As we begin this guided exercise then, whether you are a professional artist or just pursue art as a hobby, know that this energy is useful in helping you to express that idea or feeling or performance that is inside of you.

Let's begin by taking a gentle, deep breath, breathing in fresh, relaxing air and breathing out any stress or tension that you may be feeling. Very good. Now take a second breath in, relaxing as you do. Continue to breathe in a nice, rhythmic manner, breathing in relaxing fresh air and breathing out any remaining stress or tension. That's right. You may choose to keep your eyes open, or you may allow them to close at any time if you feel they are getting heavy.

Now I would like you to focus your attention on that concept, picture, music, feeling, performance, or whatever else it might be that you have been working on. Let that come into your consciousness. You may see it in your mind's eye or hear it in your head or feel it in your body. Connect with it in a manner that is most natural for you. Focus your attention on it.

Now bring in the green vibrational light of the Fourth Ray. Let it surround you. And as you feel this energy of Harmony through Conflict, focus your attention on what it is that you are looking to express. If you see a picture in your mind's eye, use this Fourth Ray to help you to see what is missing. Let it help you to see what is needed to fully express this concept or feeling.

If you are hearing the music, bring in the Fourth Ray to let you find the harmonic blending that is necessary to fully express your inner self. Continue to repeat the notes until you find the right ones.

If you are feeling that connection in your body, bring your awareness to that portion of your physical body and allow the feeling to express itself to you. Ask the feeling what it needs for completion and listen for the response. And as you focus in on the completed feeling, notice how you feel different than before. Is that what you meant to express? Is that the feeling you are looking for?

Individuals with a lot of Fourth Ray energy tend to live and focus a great amount of energy in their solar plexus, which is a very emotional chakra. They need to balance this energy by raising their energies higher, into the mind. The Fifth Ray, the Ray of Concrete Knowledge, helps to accomplish this. It naturally balances the Fourth Ray energy.

Work with this energy of the Fourth Ray until you feel that you have resolved your inner conflict. Trust the process. If you have not yet found what you think to be the best resolution of your inner conflict, continue to focus on your current project and continue to direct the Fourth Ray into your awareness. Allow it to bring you insight and perspective that you might not have had on your own. Work to balance this energy by raising it into the mind. Process the insights you receive and see if they produce the results that you want.

I will give you a minute or two to work on your own.

(Wait one minute.)

We will return shortly to regular wide-awake consciousness. But before you open your eyes and return to the present, know that you can bring back all the memories of this exercise with you. You can remember everything you experienced if that is what you so desire.

Now begin to allow your consciousness to return to the full, awake state. Take a gentle breath in, feeling the air entering your lungs. Gently begin to move your fingers and your toes, and as you do, take another gentle, deep breath. Connect once again with your arms and your legs. Allow your consciousness to more fully return to your body, and when you are ready, slowly open your eyes and return to this place and this time, feeling relaxed and alert and better than you have felt all day. Welcome back.

Take some time to allow your senses to fully focus on the outside world. Remember the insights that you have experienced and integrate them into your project. Do this exercise as often as you like until you reach your goal for the current project.

Fourth Ray Meditation: CREATING HARMONY
INSIGHTS

Insights: list as many as you can remember.

Main concepts: what is the subject matter behind the concepts?

Meaning for you: how do you interpret these insights?

How can you use this in your daily life?

Why is that helpful?

Summary and Key Concepts

- The Fourth Ray is referred to as the emotional Ray, and the energy from this Ray tends to congregate in the solar plexus. This area is also known as the third chakra.
- Conflict has the potential to lead to harmony.
- Artistic individuals tend to have a lot of Fourth Ray energy. Many artists strive to accurately express their feelings in art, music, writing, and other forms.

Learnings

- There is no way to avoid conflict in this human environment.
- We live in a reality of duality. By experiencing both extremes, we can arrive at a synthesis of experience and understanding.
- It was never meant for humankind to suffer. Suffering is simply a bad habit.
- There is a widespread belief that pain and suffering are in some ways beneficial. This is an illusion. Learn to create with grace and ease instead.

CHAPTER 10

The Fifth Ray

As you continue to read about the Rays of Attributes, I hope you will see how they do indeed help us to have our human experiences. The Fourth Ray helps all those who we would broadly call artists. This Fifth Ray is referred to as the Mental Ray and as such benefits all the scientists on our planet. The Sixth Ray helps another entire group of individuals. These are indeed broad, general categories. The way we individually draw on them and mix and weave them together provides plenty of opportunity for our individual, personal experiences.

Here is the introduction to the Fifth Ray.

Now, the Fifth Ray. The Fifth Ray is an orange, an orange vibration, and it is known as the vibration and energy of pure intelligence, of Concrete Knowledge. The great scientists on your planet hold a great deal of this energy. The great concepts for your planet flow through this energy. Individuals in this energy are able to conceptualize. They are able to synthesize. They are able to take apart a concept and put it back together and see the purposeful meaning as it pertains to life on Earth.

For those few individuals that can hold this vibration, these new concepts become available. As new principles come down through this Ray to your Earth, they are available in many locations to those individuals that have raised their vibration and can hold it at this level and accept the wisdom that flows. This is a very mental energy and is quite available on your planet as so many are living in their mental energies, sometimes stuck there. This energy is quite beneficial for those that are earthbound in their energies. It can be used quite effectively to balance and lift them when planted too firmly.

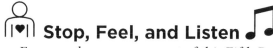 **Stop, Feel, and Listen** ♪♪

Everyone has some amount of this Fifth Ray within them. There are times when the ability to access higher levels of pure intelligence benefits us all. Please take two minutes now to feel this energy and then evaluate how and when it can be of help to you.

Allow yourself to relax into the seat you are sitting in. You should be seated for this. Take a couple of gentle, rhythmic breaths, breathing in the relaxing and refreshing fresh air and exhaling out any tension or stress that you may be feeling. Close your eyes and imagine a beautiful round ball of orange energy. See yourself getting closer and closer until you actually make contact with it and move into it. From the inside of the ball, feel yourself totally surrounded by this energy. Now allow your mind to expand and reach out. Do this for two minutes.

Once again, write down below any insights that may have occurred to you while you were processing this information.

I hope you had the opportunity to allow your consciousness to expand and work with this energy. Perhaps you got some instant insight. If you didn't, maybe you will find something of great interest in the immediate future. Or perhaps you may have to sit longer with this energy and develop your own technique to work with the energy of the Fifth Ray. If you are an individual with a lot of Fourth Ray energy, use the Fifth Ray to balance your energy. See if it makes a difference.

 Discussion

The Fifth Ray is an energy of pure intelligence. I must admit that the Team does not frequently speak of pure intelligence. There is a great deal of discussion about consciousness, but I feel that intelligence is a particular characteristic of consciousness. I'll have more to say about consciousness when we discuss the Tenth Ray.

The Fifth Ray is called the Ray of Concrete Knowledge. It is the energy of new concepts and innovation. The Team indicates that the great scientists and thinkers of our time hold a lot of this energy. We all have some of this energy. We may not think of ourselves as great thinkers, but that doesn't mean that we don't have some of this energy especially when we seek to understand the bigger picture. We call upon this energy to help us deconstruct a situation or an event, and then we look for the deeper meaning, the more subtle concepts that are at work. Then we can reassemble that experience, and seeing it from a different perspective, we can use that understanding to help shape our personal reality.

As we work to raise our total vibratory level, we gain access to the higher-level Concrete Knowledge associated with this Ray. I believe that access to information in general is more tightly regulated in our time than it has been during previous great periods of civilization on the planet. I'm thinking particularly of the times of Lemuria and Atlantis. Perhaps I should just say that I hope there is more limited access to Concrete Knowledge these days than in the distant past. I believe that unrestricted access to information contributed to the destruction of Atlantis. I would hope that adjustments have been made based upon previous experiences so that different outcomes are more probable.

I find the most interesting portion of this explanation of the Fifth Ray to be "as new principles come down through this Ray to your Earth." I am curious about who decides to send these new principles our way and how the timing is determined. I think we love to believe that we are big boys and big girls and can do this by ourselves, advance humankind, but I would suggest that the evidence speaks to the contrary. We haven't yet been able to make much progress as far as advancement goes. Sure our technology keeps improving, but does our awareness of ourselves and our understanding of our multidimensional being keep up with that progress?

I believe that just as each and every individual on this planet has helpers from other dimensions—guides, teachers, angels, God, and so on—humankind as a whole has its helpers. I'm not saying that we are controlled by unforeseen forces, for the law of free will is certainly in effect in our dimension, but there is some amount of helpful guidance, perhaps nudging that goes on—kind of like the nudge you got from one of your parents when you were younger to go over and ask someone to dance at your cousin's wedding reception.

There is one more aspect of the Fifth Ray that I would like to mention. The Team says that this energy is good for people who are "earthbound in their energies." So what do you think they mean by that? Too grounded perhaps? Do any of you know folks who are too grounded, people who are so focused on everyday living and caught up in all the drama? They tend to be totally wrapped up in their emotions. I bet we all know one or two like that. So this energy is very useful to help them create more balance in their lives and maybe also in our own lives.

 ## Fifth Ray Meditation: THE BIGGER PICTURE

The Fifth Ray, the Ray of Concrete Knowledge, is also known as the Mental Ray. It is a vibrant orange-colored energy. The notable scientists of our planet hold a great deal of this energy. But what about the rest of us? This energy is available to all and can be very balancing when individuals find themselves to be too grounded in their emotions. Remember that each of us holds varying amounts of these energies of the Rays of Attributes. And while one of the Rays of Attributes is normally dominant, the others are present in amounts that can be intentionally adjusted.

One of the practical applications for this Ray then is to lift an individual out of their emotional state and move them into a more mental, thinking state. This allows an individual to focus on a certain concept and take it apart and see its true essence without the emotional distractions associated with it. This provides the opportunity to synthesize its true essence into a bigger perspective. Once this synthesis takes place, the individual can put the concept back together and add the learning into the individual's wealth of experience. As we move deeper into this exercise, I will suggest some more concrete examples of how to use this energy.

Let's begin now by getting ourselves into position. I suggest you sit in an upright position with your legs firmly on the floor or folded underneath you. Allow your arms and hands to rest gently at your sides or in your lap. You may begin with your eyes open or closed, whichever is more comfortable for you. If your eyes are open, allow them to close when they begin to feel heavy. Make sure that you will be undisturbed for the next ten minutes or so. Also make sure that you can direct your full attention to this exercise. There should be no distractions present.

As we begin to work with the Fifth Ray energy, the energy of Concrete Knowledge, focus on your breath. Take a gentle, deep breath in, breathing in pleasant, relaxing energy and exhaling out any stress or tension that you may be feeling. Take another gentle, deep breath, breathing in relaxation and exhaling out any remaining tension or stress. Very good.

Now remember that the Fifth Ray energy is a vibrant orange energy. Imagine yourself surrounded now by this beautiful, orange energy. In your mind's eye, see this orange energy all around you. You bring in this energy simply by using your intention. Direct this vibrant orange energy to surround you though your thoughts. Very good.

Focus now on some personal relationship or concept or event that you find very emotional. You may visualize it as a picture in your mind's eye. Or you may hear it as voices or sounds in your mind. Or you may feel it in your body. If you sense it in your body, bring your awareness to that part of your body now. Focus on that part.

Now surround it with this orange energy of the Fifth Ray. Separate it from any emotions you may be feeling. Begin to take it apart piece by piece.

If you are dealing with an event, play it now in slow motion understanding the deeper meaning of each frame. If you are dealing with a concept, allow yourself to see that all concepts are composed of smaller pieces. Allow yourself to become aware of what those smaller pieces are. See how they fit together.

If you are dealing with a person, allow yourself to see that person as being just like you. See them without your judgment of them, without your emotions being projected onto them. With all that stripped away, what do you see as the essence of your relationship with this person?

I'll give you a minute or two to explore this more deeply.

(Wait one minute.)

And when you achieve that insight that you have been searching for, begin to put the pieces back together again from your new perspective. Hopefully, you now have different choices to choose from when you consider how to most appropriately move forward in relation to the personal relationship, concept, or event that you have been working with in this exercise.

In just a minute, I will ask you to begin to return to your regular, wide-awake consciousness. Take this remaining time to remember all that you have experienced in today's exercise. You can bring back the full memory of all that you experienced today if you so choose.

Now take a gentle, deep breath, and as you do, begin to allow your consciousness to return to your physical body. Feel the air entering into your lungs. Gently wiggle your fingers and your toes allowing your consciousness to more fully return to your physical body. Connect once again with your arms and your legs. Take another gentle, deep breath becoming aware of the chair you are sitting in and when you are ready, slowly open your eyes and return to this place and this time feeing refreshed, relaxed, wide awake, and now feeling better than you have felt all day. Welcome back.

Repeat this exercise as often as you choose. Use it anytime you feel too grounded in your emotions.

Fifth Ray Meditation: THE BIGGER PICTURE
INSIGHTS

Insights: list as many as you can remember.

_____

_____

_____

_____

Main concepts: what is the subject matter behind the concepts?

_____

_____

_____

_____

Meaning for you: how do you interpret these insights?

_____

_____

_____

_____

How can you use this in your daily life?

_____

_____

_____

_____

Why is that helpful?

_____

_____

_____

_____

Summary and Key Concepts

- The Fifth Ray is the Ray of Concrete Knowledge. It is also referred to as the Mental Ray.
- The great scientists of our planet hold a great deal of this energy.
- The great concepts for our planet flow through this energy.

Learnings

- As new principles come down to us through this Ray, any individual who can maintain this level of energy may become aware of them. This is why new discoveries are often made at about the same time all over the planet.
- Use this energy in small amounts to help ground and balance individuals who are too emotionally involved with daily living.
- It seems that these new principles are released through conscious choice and planning. This suggests that a plan for humankind exists and is being followed.

CHAPTER 11

The Sixth Ray

think it is fair to say that of all the Rays we have the least amount of information about the Sixth Ray. The curious part about the information that we do have is that it first presents the somewhat negative aspect of too much of the Sixth Ray. Older texts about the Rays have often discussed the positive and the negative aspects of each Ray. I'm sure that there is a balance for the Rays as there is for most things, and I can see how too much of one Ray can create a very deliberate outcome. I see the purpose in that. I'm just not sure that I would label certain outcomes as positive or negative. That seems like a judgment to me, and the Team certainly doesn't discuss the effects of too much of the Sixth Ray as being good or bad. They simply make the statement that too much has a certain effect.

> *The Sixth Ray is a Ray of Devotion and Idealism, and you can visualize it as indigo blue. The Sixth Ray focuses—has a very precise focus in its energy, and people that carry a lot of this energy tend to be obsessive. It has addictive qualities in regards to religion. It can create an energy of zealous belief. It can be used to put things on automatic.*
>
> *You can bring this Ray in, focus on it, envision it growing lighter, for this energy is a very heavy energy in your earthly environment; it tends to cling. Yet used by raising it up in a lighter, less addictive vibration, it can help focus your intentions and your goals, your objectives.*

As the Rays move through the dimensions into our third dimension, they each take on a certain vibration, a certain frequency, as well as other characteristics such as color. Each Ray vibrates within a range, and as the Team is here suggesting, this heavy energy of the Sixth Ray can be raised up to a lighter vibration. The way to raise this or any energetic vibration is to release any and all fear that is associated with it.

When we focus our attention, it is usually to achieve some goal or some desired outcome. There may be some trepidation associated with achieving a specific goal. For some reason, many of us avoid change. The fear of change is strong in us. Yet change happens in our lives all the time. Many are just comfortable pretending that it isn't happening. Others may feel that the change is out of their control, and they are not responsible for it.

Identify and release the fear, whether it is related to change or something else, and you raise the energy to a higher vibration.

This notion of raising energetic frequencies is very important because when you think of it, that is what we are all actually doing now. We all have the opportunity to raise our individual vibrations, and when we do, we help the planet raise its individual energetic vibration. Think of all the fear that you have experienced in this current lifetime. Now consider the fear that everyone else has experienced. It is easy to see how all of that fear can be weighing us all down.

Why is it important to raise our individual energetic levels? Energy is information, and as the information passes into the lower and heavier vibrations, there is a reduction in the information that reaches us. Whenever we can work with energy at a higher vibration, we in essence have more information to work with.

The second paragraph indicates that when you raise up the frequency of the Sixth Ray, it can be very useful in helping us to focus our intentions. The Team has mentioned the benefit of learning to focus our attention several times.

There is a clear connection between being able to focus our attention and our ability to manifest whatever we choose to have in our lives. The Team gives a further comment on how focusing our attention helps to direct the energy of the Rays as they flow through our physical bodies.

> From the center of Source flow all Twelve Rays, which are transmuted into liquid light and enter the body through the glands and nervous channels. This concentrated electronic energy flows wherever your attention directs it. The mind's attention, however, is distracted by thought, feeling, sight, hearing—all the senses. We cannot emphasize enough to the individual what power you have at your command when you have gained full control of your attention. This light becomes colored by whatever Ray or point of integration the personality is expressing through thought, feeling, and one's ability to assimilate and integrate.
>
> Here lies one's responsibility as a creator as well as the means to correct or purify whatever has been wrongly created. In other words, you have the ability to rewrite your script even though all of creation is played out in the eternal now, without time, space, or causation—one of the many advantages of expressing dense physical embodiment.

I think about my "responsibility as a creator," and I wonder how often I act in a responsible manner as I am creating my reality. But perhaps that is too literal of an interpretation. What is my responsibility as a creator? Do any of us really take responsibility for our creations, or do we just walk away from them and let others deal with our creations? I can see an entire series of meditations just around this concept. Am I a responsible creator? I bet that would lead to some interesting insights.

You not only have the potential to create faster but also the ability to "rewrite your script." According to the Team, you can "correct or purify whatever has been wrongly created." How would you go about identifying something that you have wrongly created? How does knowing that you have the power to recreate what you have wrongly created make you feel? It feels very empowering to me.

These aspects of the Sixth Ray give me plenty of incentive to spend time to understand how all this responsible creator stuff works. Let's begin with a simple connection to the Sixth Ray. Take two minutes and stop and feel the energy of this most interesting Ray.

Stop, Feel, and Listen

Allow yourself to relax and sit comfortably in your seat. Take a gentle deep breath and imagine the incoming air to be filled with relaxing, calming energy. When you exhale, breath out any stress or tension that you may be feeling. Now invite the indigo blue energy of the Sixth Ray to be with you. You may imagine it surrounding you, or you may simply feel it already there with you. As you connect with this Ray, allow your mind to focus on a new goal or intention. When you have received an acceptable new goal or intention, return to your regular waking state.

Write down below any insights that may have occurred to you while you were processing this information.

When you have some more time, work with this Ray to help you focus any of your intentions or goals. If you feel any resistance within yourself, go inside and use the First Ray to identify the resistance. Is it fear? It is something else? Then call upon the Third Ray to help you understand how to move beyond the resistance. Use the Third Ray to show you the steps you need to take to move forward.

Discussion

What I find most curious about the Sixth Ray passage is that the Team is very specific. They are not being judgmental; they are simply stating what they know to be their reality. This Ray has "addictive qualities in regards to religion." I think we can all conjure up images of religious figures who are filled with fervor. They seem driven to share their experience of religion with the entire world, some of the time in total disregard for the other person's personal beliefs. I myself may have been filled with too much of this energy in a prior life experience. The word zealot seems to resonate with me curiously enough.

The Team also talks about bringing this energy in and raising it up to a lighter vibration where it is not as addictive. When we do that, we can use the energy of the Sixth Ray to help us focus our attention. And when we focus our attention, we can visualize our personal goals that will help us to create the reality we came here to experience.

Most likely, you have had some prior experience with religious devotion, and you or someone you know may have allowed that devotion to become obsessive. Think of all the crusades or the inquisitions or even the witch burnings. And there are plenty of more recent examples. Religious wars have been around for a long time. You can take that energy from those experiences and raise it up to help release you from prior, obsessive emotions. Then you can use the higher-level energy of this Ray to help you achieve your goals for this life experience.

 # Sixth Ray Meditation: FOCUS

Let's begin by taking a gentle, deep breath, breathing in fresh, relaxing air and breathing out any stress or tension that you may be feeling. Very good. Now take a second breath in, relaxing as you do. Continue to breathe in a nice, rhythmic manner, breathing in relaxing fresh air and breathing out any remaining stress or tension. That's right. You may choose to keep your eyes open, or you may allow them to close at any time if you feel they are getting heavy.

The Sixth Ray is referred to as the Ray of Devotion and Idealism. You can visualize its color as a beautiful, indigo blue. Sixth Ray energy helps you to focus on your goals and intentions. And when it is balanced, it is used very constructively to promote devotion and idealism. Too much of this energy, however, can cause extremism, compulsiveness, and even zealotry.

So it is very important when you work with this energy to raise it up to a lighter level—to clarify it and purify it through your intentions. Allow your intentions to be driven by love and not by the lower emotions of fear and anger and suffering.

Use this energy to focus on your intentions and to create your goals. Many individuals wonder why their lives are not different. They wonder why it is so difficult for them to manifest what their hearts desire. If you want to become a real estate broker, a massage therapist, a pilot, or perhaps a doctor or lawyer, it important to set that as your goal first. Then with your intention, you can make choices like attending school and passing certification examinations that will lead to your successfully achieving those goals.

As you raise this energy of the Sixth Ray up through the purity of your intentions, it helps you to focus on that which you wish to manifest in your life. So allow me to suggest that you consider a goal that perhaps has been out of reach in the past. Perhaps you thought it was unattainable.

Go ahead now and pick an appropriate goal for today.

(Wait one minute.)

Working with the energy of this Sixth Ray, focus now on achieving the goal that you just selected. Allow this energy of the Sixth Ray to lead you to clarity. Allow it to give you a clear focus on your objective. I'll give you a few minutes to think about this now.

(Wait three minutes.)

We will return shortly to regular wide-awake consciousness. But before you open your eyes and return to the present, know that you can bring back all the memories of this exercise with you. You can remember everything you experienced if that is what you so desire.

Now begin to allow your consciousness to return to the full, awake state. Take a gentle breath in, feeling the air entering your lungs. Gently begin to move your fingers and your toes, and as you do, take another gentle deep breath. Connect once again with your arms and your legs. Allow your consciousness to more fully return to your body, and when you are ready, slowly and gently open your eyes and return to this place and this time, feeling relaxed, alert, and better than you have felt all day. Welcome back.

I hope that you have been able to set some goals for yourself. But more importantly, I hope you appreciate how critical it is to set goals in order to achieve what you want to experience in your life. Please take some time to write down your insights.

Sixth Ray Meditation: FOCUS
INSIGHTS

Insights: list as many as you can remember.

Main concepts: what is the subject matter behind the concepts?

Meaning for you: how do you interpret these insights?

How can you use this in your daily life?

Why is that helpful?

Summary and Key Concepts

- The Sixth Ray is the Ray of Devotion and Idealism. People with a lot of this energy tend to be obsessive.
- It has addictive qualities when it comes to religion.
- In its lighter, less addictive vibration, it can help focus your attention and your goals, your objectives.

Learnings

- There are quite a few individuals with a lot of this energy these days.
- We cannot emphasize enough the importance of learning to focus your attention, to consciously focus the energies of your thoughts and feelings, and direct that energy through love.
- We all have responsibility for what we create. What we have wrongly created can be corrected.

CHAPTER 12

The Seventh Ray

The Seventh Ray has typically been known as the Ray of Ceremonial Order or Magic. It has also been known as the Violet Flame, and in this context has been associated with the Ascended Master Saint Germain. Just to eliminate confusion if you have not heard of Saint Germain before, the "saint" in his name is there because he had a French heritage in his last incarnation, and that name has been kept. He is not a saint in the Christian sense of the word.

The Team refers to the Seventh Ray as the Gateway into Awareness. This represents a major shift in understanding the Seventh Ray energy. It is an updated explanation of the Ray's energy, and it helps us to better understand how to work with it. In our first introduction to the Seventh Ray, the purpose of the Ray was explained, and Julie and I were also given the technique for using it.

And now the Seventh Ray ... hmm ... the Seventh Ray is a violet, a violet energy that we call the Gateway into Awareness. It is the energy that is used to dissolve the weightiness of past experience and transmute that energy up into a higher vibration so that you might advance in your evolution of Spirit. You may picture this in meditation as a violet flame and move it down through the denser energies, through your chakras, raising them up, opening them to the grander, greater expression of what you know yourself to be.

Once again, we are presented with the notion of raising our energetic level to "advance the evolution of Spirit." The Seventh Ray has the ability to help us to "dissolve the weightiness of past experience." And what is that weightiness? It is the lower-level emotions of fear, pain, and anger, among others, that we carry with us. No wonder the Team refers to the Seventh Ray as the Gateway into Awareness.

As we release these lower-level experiences from our pasts, we raise our energetic levels, and this opens us to different perspectives that afford new and different insights and awareness.

The Team continued in the same session with this information.

> *Saint Germain watches over this Ray.*

This is the Violet Flame of Saint Germain?

> *It is his Ray.*

It is the Ray we experienced at Mount Shasta, and that Ray has been working with us ever since.

> *It came to you, was open to you before that time, but you opened to it. You opened to it. You accepted this energy on Mount Shasta. You were in the river of this energy. You've flown through its gates. It works through you. All these energies that we have spoken about flow through you. Becoming aware of them is simply a way to raise that consciousness to enlighten you to the power that you work with, that you avail yourself of. You choose, every moment, the energies you bring to your being, and by so doing, you affect the energies of everything in your reality.*

Saint Germain has long been associated with the Seventh Ray and with healing work in general. As I come to have a better understanding of the nature of healing, the manner in which I work with the Seventh Ray shifts. Healing has been thought of for many generations as the curing of disease. But before modern medicine embraced science as the source of all healing, healing was considered an art form, and practitioners were more interested in the bigger picture of the client's well-being.

Disease represented an imbalance, and the local medicine man or woman—by whatever name he or she was called—would seek to reestablish the sick person's balance. This could be a physical imbalance, an energetic imbalance, a spiritual imbalance, or any combination of the preceding. As I rediscover the nature of wellness and once again practice wellness as an art form, I understand how useful this energy of the Seventh Ray is in helping to reestablish balance in my clients and myself.

The Team gets very specific when they discuss pain and suffering, and they provide us guidance in using the Seventh Ray to release our long-held habits of creating pain and suffering in our earthly experiences.

> *In this experience that you are having on your planet, unlearn—unlearn what difficulty is to you. Difficulty in your life and your experience is an*

illusion. It does not exist. It exists only from your creation on your planet. Spiritually, you know this. Emotionally, you are confused. Mentally, you resist. You are perplexed on how all things fit. Humanity tells you, has created for you, an illusion that mankind must suffer, that difficulty must be part of your experience. This is a great illusion. Unlearn the habit of difficulty. Find the joy in every moment, in every experience. Find the ease as you release. Affirm to yourself: I do not suffer. Let it bring to your awareness each resistance and allow that resistance to float away. Do this as you use the Rays. Affirm as you draw through you, as you integrate. Allow that resistance to make itself a known energy and allow it to release. Then replace it with the joy, the true nature of who you are.

I remember listening to the notion that difficulty is a habit, and I was overwhelmed by this insight. Wow, we all have habits, but I never thought of difficulty as a habit. Do we really make things harder for ourselves? What do we stand to gain by making things harder than they really are? Do we benefit because of our individual pain and suffering? Can we create more sympathy from those around us if our lives are filled with more hardships than someone else's? The plain and simple answer to all of these questions is yes.

Looking at difficulty as a habit, how do we go about breaking this very entrenched, habituated, behavioral pattern? When an individual is ready to release what might be coined the "no pain, no gain" syndrome, the Team suggests using the Seventh Ray but not just in releasing the habit of difficulty. We can also use it to help embrace the grandness of who we are, for we all resist stepping into the larger vision of our greatness.

The Violet Flame—call on the Violet Flame when you are ready, when those you work with are ready to acknowledge the resistance that they hold, when they are ready to accept what they are. You may find that it is hard to believe that most people [we] would dare say most people on your planet have yet to agree, to acknowledge their own perfection, their potential. They do not understand they do not have to suffer. They do not understand they do not have to live in difficulty.

Jesus never desired to suffer, never desired for His people, all of mankind, to acknowledge any suffering from Him. When you release this illusion, you open a door to releasing all discomfort, all pain. You open a new door to draw in more love, more light. We have an opportunity here in this life, not the next—in this life, in this experience—to be in unconditional love, to understand the joy, the simplicity, the harmony.

We all have experienced resistance when we have attempted to move forward. Think about those big decisions that we make. Do I take this new job? Is this the right new house for us? Is it time for me to end this relationship? There are so many times when we embrace resistance, and very often it slows us down or impedes us altogether. The status quo may not be the optimal situation, but how do we know something new and different will not be worse?

It is fine for anyone to want to stay exactly where they are. It is fine to hold on to your beliefs. But when they are no longer working for you, you have the opportunity to examine them and move beyond if you feel that is the desired solution for you. Once you make the commitment to move beyond your current situation, use the Seventh Ray to help release your resistance to change. Use the Seventh Ray to help you embrace that grander vision of who you really are.

The Team's comments about the suffering of Jesus are very thought-provoking. I feel this is not the place to really comment about the impact of their meaning. I'll leave it up to you, the reader, to spend as much time as you wish contemplating their comments.

Stop, Feel, and Listen

Once again clear everything off your lap. Closing your eyes, take a gentle, deep relaxing breath. Focus on your breathing as you establish a nice, rhythmic breathing pattern. As you breathe in, imagine you are breathing in relaxing, soothing energy. And with each exhalation, breathe out any stress or tension that you may be feeling. Envision your seven chakras as circles, sort of like dinner plates stacked one above the other, starting with the root chakra at the base of your spine and moving all the way up to the crown chakra. Now, right above your crown chakra, envision a shaft of violet light, a shaft of violet energy moving down towards you. Allow it to move into the crown chakra and then direct it to continue to move down into each and every one of the seven major chakras. And when it reaches the final chakra, the root chakra, allow it to continue to move down through your legs and flow into the ground. And now take two minutes and feel the energy of this Ray.

Take the time again to write down below any insights that may have occurred to you while you were processing this information.

When you set your intention on releasing the old emotions that hold you back, you can visualize the Seventh Ray as heating up those emotional energies to such a temperature that the energy is actually transmuted. This process used to be referred to as "incinerating the energy," but it is more accurate to describe this process as transmuting the energy to a higher vibration, a lifting up of the energy. The Team sometimes refers to this process as a cleansing.

This process of transmuting lower-level energies involves the energies from this lifetime, but you can go back as far as you choose to transmute energies that still hold you back. The following is a brief exchange with the Team about this process.

I understand that feeling alone is a choice. And I wonder if, in all those past lives I have endured being alone, it [feeling alone] has become a friend of mine that I must say goodbye to.

Endurance is your choice. Aloneness comes from recognition of a separation. You now at this point recognize union, connection. Yet old experience, going back lifetime after lifetime exists within and must be cleansed.

Ah, it must be cleansed.

Use the Rays.

The Violet Flame?

Use the Seventh, the Eighth, and the Ninth—these Rays to cleanse and to recognize and set a new focus, a new understanding.

 Discussion

The Seventh Ray is the Violet Flame. It is associated with Saint Germain who is most often described as an Ascended Master. He is also commonly associated with the healing arts, kind of like a patron saint of the healing arts, no pun intended.

Guy Ballard, who claims to have met Saint Germain while hiking on Mount Shasta in the 1930s, went on to form the "I AM" movement. Mark and Elizabeth Clare Prophet wrote about the Violet Flame extensively in the mid and later parts of the twentieth century. My feeling is that those were messages for that time. What I would generally refer to as New Age material needs to be updated for this time. The energies have shifted substantially, and what was relevant then is not necessarily relevant today.

With that background, we used to think about the Violet Flame as an energy that incinerates lower-level emotions that are ready to be discarded. The Team has recently clarified the use of the Seventh Ray. They suggest that the Seventh Ray can be used to transmute these lower-level energies to a lighter level and thereby lift them up so that we can move beyond into new understanding.

I have included a very interesting meditation with the Seventh Ray. It involves the Merkaba, the Merkaba Valley (which is a real valley on the planet), and your guides and teachers. I am going ask you to build an individual Merkaba energetically, and you are going to do it by envisioning yourself in the Merkaba Valley. The Merkaba Valley has six mountaintops, and you may see them as being snow covered or not. On each mountain peak, there will be one of your guides or teachers, and they might appear to you as totally energetic beings, or you may see them as you normally would. Each one will be directing the Seventh Ray towards you. You will be in the center of the valley.

 ## Seventh Ray Meditation: THE VIOLET FLAME

As we begin this meditation for the Seventh Ray, I'd like you to get comfortable in your chair. If you have anything on your lap, please put it on the floor now. Just gently relax your hands either in your lap or at your sides. Have your feet resting comfortably beneath you, either on the floor or folded in some way. Take a relaxing, deep breath, and as you exhale, breathe out any stress or anxiety that you may be feeling. Continue to focus on your breath and maintain a gentle, rhythmic breathing pattern. Good.

Now I would like you to see yourself in your sacred place, that place where you go to be quiet, to be peaceful, to be safe. This is the place where you can easily connect with your guides and your teachers or your angels or whoever else joins you when you do your sacred work. Ask them now to join you and to be part of this meditation using the Seventh Ray.

Envision yourself in a beautiful, lush, green valley with a sparkling, clear stream running through it. As you look around, you notice that there are six mountain peaks of varying elevations. Three of the peaks are taller than the others and they might even appear to be snow covered. Take a deep, gentle breath and breathe in this refreshing, clean mountain air. Continue to breath nice and rhythmically.

Bring your awareness to your crown chakra, the top of your head and connect with the beautiful violet energy that is there. This is the energy of the Creator, of the Source, which you are always connected to. Now invite that energy to descend into your physical body. Allow it to move through your third eye, the sixth chakra. Allow it to continue to descend moving past your throat chakra. And allow it to come to reside in your heart center, your fourth chakra. Now to this energy we would like today to give the intention of love and healing, kindness, compassion, forgiveness, higher self-awareness, and gratitude.

Now bring your awareness to your root chakra at the base of your spine. Envision and connect with the beautiful red energy of Mother Earth. This energy is also with you all the time. Now invite that energy to move up into your body. Allow it to move up past your second chakra, your sacral chakra. Allow it to continue to rise through your abdomen. Allow it to continue to move past your solar plexus and bring it also into your heart center. Now to this energy we wish to also give intention. So to this energy we give our intention for today of love and healing, connection to Mother Earth, loving relationships, higher self-esteem, abundance in all things, and gratitude.

Now allow these two energies to come together and, as they do, allow them to expand. Allow them to totally surround you, creating your personal, energetic Merkaba. See yourself in the middle of this Merkaba and now bring in the luminescent aqua-blue energy of the Second Ray, the energy of Love and Wisdom, and begin to wrap it around you starting at your head and moving now down around your shoulders. Continue to wrap it around your abdomen and your waist, moving down now around your legs and your feet until you are totally wrapped up in this energy, until it has formed a sort of cocoon all around you.

Focus your attention now on the six mountain peaks, and you will notice that there is an energetic being on each one of the peaks, and each being is violet in color. Each being is focusing the Violet Flame energy, and they direct this energy towards you. And as they do, they create another larger Merkaba totally out of the energy of the Seventh Ray. And you find yourself in the middle of this Merkaba also.

Envision a column of violet energy descending on you from above. Allow this energy to make contact with your crown chakra and, as it does, allow any lower-level energy to be transmuted and raised up by this energy of the Seventh Ray. Any time you felt disconnected from the Source, any time you felt you were on your own, allow that energy to be raised up and transmuted, knowing that you are always connected to the energy of the Creator.

When you are ready, allow the violet energy of the Seventh Ray to move down into your sixth chakra. And here allow it to raise up, to transmute any lower-level energy you might have related to any beliefs that you have difficulty connecting with the inner realms, that you have difficulty connecting with your guides and your teachers, that your ability to connect with these inner realms is somehow blocked. Allow those beliefs and emotions to be transmuted by the Violet Flame.

Continue to allow the energy of the Violet Flame to move down and allow it to enter your throat chakra, your fifth chakra. Here you can release any beliefs or emotions that prevent you from speaking your truth. Release them to the Seventh Ray and use the Ray to raise up that energy so high that you now feel empowered to speak your truth in a loving and constructive manner. Feel your confidence increase. Remember also that the energy of the fifth chakra is about following your soul's purpose, your soul's plan. So release any doubts or experiences that you feel have blocked you from following your soul's purpose. Allow the Violet Flame to help you transmute this energy and help you refocus on your soul's journey.

Now allow the Seventh Ray energy to move into your heart center, your fourth chakra. This is your heart center, your center of love. Allow the Seventh Ray to help you transmute any feeling of not being loved, of not being worthy of love. Remember that you are always connected to the Source, and that means you are always connected to love. Your feelings of not being loved are merely an illusion. Now allow any such illusions to be lifted up through the awareness of your constant connection. Use the Seventh Ray to help you reestablish this connection to love if you need to.

When you are ready, allow the energy of the Seventh Ray to continue to move through you into your third chakra, your solar plexus. This is your center of personal power. Anytime you have felt that you were not able to do something or were not strong enough or good enough—allow those feelings to be transmuted by the energy of the Seventh Ray. Allow those memories and emotions to be cleansed of any doubt or fear, and as they are cleansed, they are raised up by this energy of the Violet Flame.

Continue to allow the Violet Flame to descend into your second chakra, your sacral chakra. Connect with your relationships and any relationships that you feel are not loving. Allow them to be transmuted and raised up by the energy of the Seventh Ray. If there are any relationships that you need to let go of, raise up the energy of those relationships and honor them as you release them and move forward.

Allow the energy of the Violet Flame to move now into your root chakra at the base of your spine. Any energies that have held you in fear of your survival—raise them up using the Seventh Ray. Any energies or beliefs that there is not enough to support you—allow the Violet Flame to transmute that energy knowing you are constantly provided for just as the birds in the trees are provided for. Know that you are watched over and that any feeling of lack or scarcity is purely an illusion.

Now allow the energy of the Seventh Ray to flow through your legs and your feet and see this beautiful energy flow into Mother Earth where she absorbs it and uses it to transmute energy just as you do.

Now bring in the energy of the Eighth Ray, a green and violet energy, to cleanse your chakras. See it as a shaft or column of light descending upon you. Allow it to move through you, starting with your crown chakra and moving through each chakra, and as it does, it cleanses and balances each and every chakra. And let it flow all the way down into Mother Earth cleansing and balancing as it flows through you.

Now take a minute and feel yourself cleansed and refreshed and invigorated. Feel yourself at this new energetic level and hold this higher frequency. Become acquainted with this higher energetic level and make it your own.

(Wait one minute.)

In a minute I am going to invite you to return to your room. Take this remaining time to thank your guides and your teachers for their assistance today. And when you thank them for their help today, listen to how they respond to you. Pay particular attention to what they say back to you. Take a minute and allow yourself to feel their energy and the energy of their words.

(Wait one minute.)

Now once again notice the beauty of this valley. Feel your new level of vibration. How good does it feel to have transmuted all of that old energy to this new, higher level?

And when you are ready, I'd like you to take a gentle, deep breath. Breathe in the clear, clean, refreshing air of this lush valley and, as you do, gently exhale, becoming aware once again of your breath. And as you continue gently breathing in and out, allow your consciousness to begin to return to your physical body. And as you feel your consciousness slowly returning to your physical body, gently move your fingers and your toes. And as you are moving your fingers and your toes, allow yourself to connect once again with your arms and your legs. Allow your total consciousness to now return to your physical body and, when you are ready, gently open your eyes and return to this place and this time. Welcome back.

Seventh Ray Meditation: THE VIOLET FLAME
INSIGHTS

Insights: list as many as you can remember.

_____

_____

_____

_____

Main concepts: what is the subject matter behind the concepts?

_____

_____

_____

_____

Meaning for you: how do you interpret these insights?

_____

_____

_____

_____

How can you use this in your daily life?

_____

_____

_____

_____

Why is that helpful?

_____

_____

_____

_____

It is likely that this experience has been much different for you than our previous journeying. You might have been deeply impacted by the connection you established with your guides and teachers. Perhaps you are still feeling the connection with the energies of the Seventh Ray? Maybe you were so wrapped up in the total experience that you simply wanted to stay there in the valley?

If this was the first time you have felt the presence of your guides and teachers and had an opportunity to converse with them, congratulations. I hope you felt totally supported and loved. If you have yet to feel their presence, don't worry. This process is different for everyone. Some individuals never see or hear their guides and teachers. Instead, over time they develop a feeling when they are present. The good news is you can return to the valley anytime you want and connect with your guides and teachers and the Seventh Ray.

Let me point out that, of course, it is not necessary to travel to the Merkaba Valley to work with the Seventh Ray. You can just as easily be sitting in your favorite meditation space at home and just bring the Violet Flame to you there. I suggest you try it both ways. And of course, there are many other ways to work with the Seventh Ray. Have fun constructing your own scenarios.

Now that you have worked with the energy of the seven Rays, it is time to move on to the Rays of Soul Integration. In the following chapters, I will review the Eighth Ray, which I kind of snuck in there during the meditation just now. Then we will move onto Rays Nine and Ten. This is where the new and exciting energies are. I'll have a few new concepts to share with you like the Body of Light and the Spiritual Microtron. Microtron? What is a Spiritual Microtron? Sounds like something from a 1950s science-fiction movie. I know it has a funny sounding name, but I assure you it is fabulous.

Then from there we will move on and experience the Eleventh and Twelfth Rays. These are referred to as the Bridge to New Awareness and the New Awareness.

Just in case you are wondering where all this is going, what this is all leading up to, it is leading up to a new focus, a new understanding. This new focus and new understanding is what the Rays of Soul Integration, Rays Eight through Twelve, are all about.

Summary and Key Concepts

- Use the Seventh Ray, the Violet Flame, to dissolve the weightiness of past experience.
- Unlearn what difficulty is to you. Difficulty in your life and experience is an illusion. Unlearn the habit of difficulty. It is a bad habit.
- Disease is more than we have been lead to believe.
- We do not need to suffer.
- Joy is part of our true nature.

Learnings

- We play an active role in our well-being.
- You can believe that disease is just the result of random chance. Or you can understand and acknowledge that you have a hand in its appearance.
- When you take responsibility for what you create, then you can create wellness to replace disease.
- Most disease is the result of our toxic thinking and our toxic beliefs. Changing these leads to wellness.
- Everything can be healed.
- When you dissolve the weightiness of past experience, you raise your personal energetic level.

Soul Integration

"There are five—five additional that are a blending of the lower seven. They are not chakra oriented, although there is a connection. The blending of the top five [the Rays of Soul Integration], the additional five is the beginning of your integration, your soul blending with your physical being, a blending of your emotional and mental bodies as never before. It is energy that works with an individual to bring you closer into awareness and understanding of the reality of your greatness and works with your planet, as your planet breathes, integrating its oneness to the dimension that it resides in and the other dimensions that await to be realized in its awakening. It works within your solar system with the life force of your galaxy. And it works with each cell, with each heart center, creating new life at ALL levels. It is an endless reservoir creating and cleansing and creating NEW."

CHAPTER 13

The Rays of Soul Integration

Several years ago I became very interested in turtles. When I think of sea turtles, I think of these large creatures gliding gracefully through the vast oceans. They don't seem to be like other inhabitants of the seas—no fins, no gills, no sleek bodies. They are usually solitary travelers. I can't recall ever seeing turtles swimming in a group. They need to breathe, so they must surface every now and then. They have the ability to go onto land and can survive there for long periods. And of course, the most distinctive feature of the turtle is that it wears its skeleton on the outside in the form of a shell. It also uses the shell as protection. It can withdraw into its hard fortress to defend itself. It is this distinctive ability to retreat inside that I think was resonating most with me.

I went down to St. John for my daughter's wedding a few years ago, and I was hopeful I might see some ocean turtles around the reefs. My son told me that he had seen turtles several times while swimming around the reefs that are accessible from shore. I even went on a chartered snorkeling trip hoping to see some turtles. Unfortunately, there was no live encounter with these magnificent creatures. I returned from my trip with one of those brightly painted ceramic turtles that still delights me today.

I became so interested in turtles that I started collecting turtle figurines. I acquired a pretty, green, jade turtle at a New Age show in Charlotte. I also purchased a yellow turtle night-light that I use in my bedroom. I began to notice turtles everywhere. Then one day I asked myself, "What's with all the turtles?"

The metaphor of the turtle hiding in its shell is too blatant not to recognize. Was I hiding in my shell? Was I being defensive? What was I afraid of? The simple answer is that I was afraid of myself. My energy was collapsing inward. It was shrinking rather than expanding. Keep in mind that Julie and I had been communicating with a group of beings from a different dimension for several years at that point. You might think that this would empower me rather than cause me to seek some safe place.

Sometimes the Team speaks as one voice, and sometimes they speak as individuals. I have casual conversations with them about all kinds of topics, my soul's purpose, the meaning of love, how the universe works. They even give me love-life advice.

They also remind me every time we converse that I am a multidimensional being and that what I understand myself to be is but a mere glimmer of who I really am. And for some reason, that scares me. It scares me to think that I may have lived a life as a king or some notable historical figure who associated with other notable, historical figures. So I hide in my shell, and I play it small. I let myself get distracted by all the drama of everyday life. I try to convince myself that this is what life is really all about, all the while knowing that there is a greater reality.

This greater reality seems foreign to me. I know the Team is real. I talk to them and converse with them just as if they were sitting in front of me. And yet they are not in front of me. They tell me of past lives, of our experiences together in those lifetimes, yet I have no recollection of them. They tell me of experiences I have had in other dimensions. It all seems so foreign to me, and yet I believe it all.

Why do I believe them? Because there is an energy that I feel every time we talk. They surround me with their love, and I feel it. Their words are more than just words. Their words have unbelievable depth to them. They have feeling. They have love.

Most of all, their words have integrity. They honor me, and they honor Julie. They honor all of us who are incarnated on the planet now. They never have a negative comment or share a negative thought. Their messages come from a place of love. They tell us of the power of love. They tell us that love is all there is. They tell us that there is one Source, the Source of all that is. The Source is love. They tell us that all of this, all of what we perceive with our physical senses comes from the one Source. It is channeled down through our higher selves, through our souls, through our spirits, into this dimension. They tell us that we are constantly connected to our multidimensional selves. And I believe them. Yet I still wanted to hide in my shell.

What do these higher Rays offer? To start with, they helped me see that it is safe to come out of my shell. We— you, me, and everyone else—are not alone. We are constantly supported and loved and watched over. We are powerful creators beyond our wildest understandings. And we have free will. Those who support us from the unseen realities will never do anything that infringes upon our free will. That is why they wait. They wait for us to decide that we are ready. They wait for us to come out of our shells and experience this dimension differently than we have ever experienced it before.

Some individuals will continue to play it small, and that is alright. There will be other opportunities to choose differently. Others will embrace the change and be the explorers of this new awareness.

This section provides information about the journey from what we have known in the past—what we have considered real and normal—to what we can create in the present, in the here and now. How do we bridge that gap? Where do we find the courage to leave the past behind? Who is here to help us come out of our shells?

This is what the Rays of Soul Integration are all about. These higher Rays help us connect to our multidimensional selves. They help us connect with our supporters in the other dimensions. They help us to shift our perspectives and see bigger pictures. They help each of us stand in our own personal power, knowing that we have the wisdom and the love to use it to move all of humanity forward. The Rays of Soul Integration are our personal tools to be more, to experience life differently than we ever have before.

There are a few new terms that I would like to introduce here. I'm not going into a lot of detail right now. I discuss them in more detail in the Tenth Ray chapter. The Team talks about them extensively, and I'll mention them here so that they will begin to become familiar.

The first term is the "Body of Light." The Team defines the Body of Light as "that experience of self that you utilize when you leave the Earth plane." It is a part of your multidimensional self. It is not what some refer to as a mental body or our emotional body or our etheric body. These energetic bodies already surround each of us. The Body of Light is that expression of ourselves in what some might call the astral plane.

We have never before been able to bring the Body of Light into this dimension until now. But in order to do this, we must adjust our individual energetic levels in order to begin to connect with it. The preceding Rays are wonderful at helping us to do that. We can indeed connect with the Body of Light, and we now have the ability to begin to anchor it into our physical bodies in this dimension. There will be much more on this.

The next concept is the Spiritual Microtron, which is the smallest unit of energy. Everything is composed of it. Now don't get all scientific on me and say, "Well, I've never heard of that before." You won't hear about the Spiritual Microtron in any scientific journals. They don't have the equipment that can detect it yet. The Team describes the Microtron as "the spiritualization of matter."

One of the most important characteristics of the Microtron is that it has consciousness. The inference here is that since the Microtron has consciousness and all of matter is composed of the Spiritual Microtron, then all of creation has consciousness. I'm not asking you to believe that just yet. Some may think, well, of course it does. Others may think, "How does that chair have consciousness?" Well, all consciousness doesn't appear like human consciousness. Rock consciousness is rock consciousness. Chair consciousness is chair consciousness. And of course, human consciousness is human consciousness. It is not all the same, but it is still all consciousness.

This is a key concept for us to understand. One of my favorite quotes from the Team is, "For intelligence to act, there must be intelligence to be acted upon." I take that to mean that in order for us as humans (or really in any of our multidimensional expressions of ourselves) to create, there must be intelligence that understands our intentions. That intelligence is then able to deliver whatever it is that we are intending. That is key to the understanding of humankind as cocreators of our reality here on Earth. We all are participating in the creation of all that we see around us. There will be much more discussion of the Spiritual Microtron to come.

Now it is time to move into the higher Rays themselves. The Team's introduction to the higher Rays is very interesting, and I'm going to share it with you here.

> *I have come to talk to you about the higher Rays. These higher Rays are blends of the Rays you have already been given with an energy of wholeness, of luminosity added to them, of purity. They should be integrated one at a time with much care. You would be well advised to use them in the order that they are given.*

I can tell you through personal experience that this is good advice. I really didn't appreciate the wisdom in this approach when it was given. It took a while to discover what integrating each Ray means. It is easy to pass over some parts of an individual session with the Team when such interesting new information is being shared. When I go back now and read this above passage, I wish I had paid more attention to it back then. I believe it would have saved some time.

I present each Ray individually, and I encourage you to integrate each Ray one at a time and to do so using much care. These higher Rays are new for us here on this planet, and like most new things, they take some time to get to know and appreciate.

Oh by the way, shortly after this manuscript was written, I again vacationed in the Virgin Islands. This time I was successful. I swam with several sea turtles in the open ocean. I observed them feeding on the bottom sea grass, and one surfaced right in front of me to get some air. In shallower water at another location, I was able to swim along with one. What a joyful experience!

CHAPTER 14

The Eighth Ray

If you had the opportunity to do the Violet Flame meditation, you had a brief encounter with the Eighth Ray. It is part of that meditation, and I really didn't explain it before we started the meditation. Here is the Team's explanation of the Eighth Ray.

> *The Eighth Ray is a violet and green Ray, a blend of the Fourth, emotional Ray; the Seventh, physical Ray; and the Fifth, mental Ray. The energy of the Fifth Ray is used to penetrate the emotional body, to cleanse and purify. And the Seventh Ray is added to transmute this energy, to raise it up. This Ray is a cleansing Ray. Use it, bring it in, bring it in through the emotional body, to cleanse and balance.*

We refer to the Eighth Ray as the Cleansing Ray and use it in conjunction with the Seventh Ray meditation. The Team doesn't often make mention of the subtle bodies that extend beyond the physical body. This is one of the few times that they mention the emotional body. These bodies are often discussed in the writings of the ancient wisdom authors, and if you are curious about them, you can find more information in *The Finding of the Third Eye* by Vera Stanley Alder.

I would like to point out that when the Team uses the term "cleanse" in reference to energy, they are referring to the process of transmuting the energy to a higher level. They often use the term "to raise it up" to describe this process. This process of raising up the lower-level energy is key to moving into an awareness of these higher Rays.

Stop, Feel and Listen

Once again take a moment and feel the energy of this Ray, the Eighth Ray. Do this before you have had a chance to mentally process the information about it. Read this next passage and then put everything down and for two minutes visualize the energy of the Eighth Ray.

See yourself seated with your hands resting gently in front of you or at your sides. Begin a nice, rhythmic breathing by gently breathing in a relaxing, deep breath. As you exhale, feel any stress or tension that you may be feeling begin to flow out. Envision the area just around your physical body and see it in your mind. This is your emotional body. Bring the violet and green energy of the Eighth Ray into this body and allow it to cleanse and balance your emotional body. Do this by simply setting your intention. Allow this Eighth Ray energy to move into your physical body to balance and transmute the energy there. When you are ready, take a gentle, deep breath and allow your consciousness to return fully to your physical body. And when you are ready, open your eyes and return to this place and this time. Welcome back.

Once again, write down any insights that may have occurred to you while you were processing this information.

There is another aspect of the Eighth Ray that the Team has shared with us. They explain that the Eighth Ray can also be used to bring inner clarity.

I would define inner clarity as the elimination of the inner fog—the ability to see what serves you and distinguish that from what leads you further away from your goals and objectives. That sounds pretty handy. Here is a tool to help you take a more direct path to achieving whatever it is that you set out to accomplish. The following is their suggestion for using the Eighth Ray to gain greater inner clarity.

> *You may also use this [the Eighth Ray] to bring inner clarity through your third eye, your brow chakra. Do this by imagining a Ray of light, a tunnel of light coming in through your third eye. Move yourself through this tunnel of light and look beyond.*

When you look beyond, what do you see? I would suggest that you take a little more time with this exercise when you try it. Perhaps it would help to visualize your sacred place first. I recommend again that you take a little more time with this exercise.

 **Discussion**

The Team gives a deeper understanding of the Eighth Ray in the passage below. This is particularly appropriate for me, and I'm sure most of us (at one time or another) have had to leave behind a part of the past in order to move forward into something new. It may be an existing relationship, a current job, or even your hometown. What is particularly interesting to me in this next part is their use of the term "phoenix rising" because I had recently (this was given in February 2006) closed the doors to the wellness center I had opened three years earlier. I had named that wellness center Phoenix Rising.

> *You know, with death comes new life. The Eighth Ray, the Cleansing Ray, is your allowance of death to those things, those conditions that you no longer find necessary to hold. And from that, from those ashes, this Eighth Ray raises up, much like the phoenix rising, and it takes what no longer serves and from those ashes transforms and lifts and clears and creates new, new life. When humanity decides that they are ready to live at this level, the energies are there.*

You can see how the comment about the phoenix rising would have a deeper meaning for me. The Team chooses their words carefully, and those words really helped me put that entire experience into perspective. I had put a lot of time and money and love into that venture, and it was time to let it go and move forward and build something even better with the new tools at my disposal.

The truth is that if I had never opened Phoenix Rising, I wouldn't have met Julie the way I did. There might have been other opportunities to meet in some other place and time, but who can say for sure? We did meet during this time, and she opened her heart to me. We then began working with the Team, and who knows if you would even be reading this book now if all that hadn't happened within the context of my Phoenix Rising experience? I now see Phoenix Rising as a beacon that attracted Julie to me. It did what I needed it to do, and when its purpose was served, I was fine with letting it go.

The concept here is that we all at some time or other have the opportunity to put the past behind us and move forward. There are so many people dragging their pasts with them. I know I was very good at carrying my past around with me—and not just the baggage from this lifetime. I was carrying all kinds of dead weight from prior experiences. This is what these new Rays offer us. They offer the ability to move forward at a pace that would have taken lifetimes before.

Here is a meditation that you can use to find the meaning in any major life event. The Team has suggested we can use the Eighth Ray to provide clarity. This can also mean clarity in understanding why you or I have experienced a certain event in our lives. Or perhaps you are experiencing a major life event now, and you wish to have more clarity about it. Use this Ray to help you go inside and find that clarity.

Before you begin this meditation, think of an important life event that you would like greater clarity about. Or perhaps you feel that you are still holding on to the emotions surrounding some significant event. Have this in mind as you begin this meditation.

 Eighth Ray Meditation: GAINING CLARITY

As we begin this meditation for the Eighth Ray, I'd like you to get comfortable in your chair. If you have anything on your lap, please put it on the floor now. Just gently relax your hands either in your lap or at your sides. Have your feet resting comfortably beneath you, either on the floor or folded in some way. Take a relaxing, deep breath and as you exhale breathe out any stress or anxiety that you may be feeling. Continue to focus on your breath and maintain a gentle, rhythmic breathing pattern. Good.

Now I would like you to see yourself in your sacred place, that place inside where you go to be quiet, to be peaceful, to be safe. This is the place where you can easily connect with your guides and teachers or your angels or whoever else joins you when you do your sacred work. Ask them now to join you and to be part of this meditation using the Eighth Ray.

I would like you to visualize yourself there at your sacred place. See yourself there in your relaxed, comfortable position. Allow that image of yourself to become so clear that you can actually see what you are wearing. And when that image is so clear that you can actually see what you are wearing, notice your shirt or top. What color is it? What texture does it have? And after you have noticed what you are wearing on top, notice what you have on your legs. Are you wearing pants? Perhaps you are wearing shorts? Maybe a skirt or a dress? Or perhaps something else? And again notice the color and the texture.

And after you have noticed how you are dressed, I would like you to invite in that part of yourself that I refer to as your inner wisdom. Your inner wisdom has been watching over you all of your life and understands what you have experienced and why you have experienced it. So simply invite in your inner wisdom and allow it to take any shape or form that it thinks is most appropriate for today. This may be the form of a human, an animal, or perhaps even a color, shape, or feeling. Just invite it in and allow yourself to become aware of its presence.

Allow its presence to become so strong that you can actually visualize it. Allow its form to become clearer and clearer, and when its form is so clear that you can actually see it, notice its features. If it is in the form of a human, how is it dressed? If it is in the shape of an animal, what colors do you see? If it is just a form, notice the shape and size and color. If it is just a feeling, notice where you feel it in your body.

And after you have connected with your inner wisdom, ask it directly if it is indeed your inner wisdom and if it has come today to help you. If there is any response other than yes, thank it for showing up and send it away. Then invite your inner wisdom again to join you and wait to sense its presence. Repeat the question again and wait for the response. Proceed only when you have received a yes response. If you don't get a yes response after several attempts, then simply end this meditation and try again later.

Now bring in a column of violet and green light, the energy of the Eighth Ray, and allow it to surround you and your inner wisdom. Feel it move through you from head to toe. Now recall that life event about which you wish to get greater clarity. State your intention to have a better understanding of this event. Now sit back and allow the information to come to you. You may see pictures that provide clarity. Perhaps you hear words that offer information. Or perhaps you experience sensations and feelings that help you to better understand the life event that you are examining. I'll give you some time to receive that information now.

(Wait two minutes.)

If nothing comes or you are unsure of the meaning of what you have received, ask your inner wisdom to help you to make sense of it all. Again, I'll give you some time to do this.

(Wait one minute.)

Now once again envision that shaft of violet and green light coming down from above and allow it to wash over and through you. Allow it to help you let go of any final pieces of the event that you have been working with. Continue to allow it to wash over you and feel yourself becoming refreshed and rejuvenated. Allow the energy to fill you.

In a minute I am going to invite you to return to this time and this place. Take this remaining time to thank your inner wisdom for its assistance today. And when you thank it for its help today, ask if there are any additional comments that it would like to share with you. Take a minute and do this now.

(Wait one minute.)

When you are ready, I'd like you to take a gentle, deep breath. Breathe in a gentle breath of clear, clean, refreshing air and as you do gently exhale, becoming aware once again of your breath. And as you continue gently breathing in and out, allow your consciousness to begin to return to your physical body. And as you feel your consciousness slowly returning to your physical body, gently move your fingers and your toes. And as you are moving your fingers and your toes, allow yourself to connect once again with your arms and your legs. Allow your total consciousness to now return to your physical body. And when you are ready, gently open your eyes and return to this place and this time. Welcome back.

I suggest you take a few moments and fill in the following worksheet with the details of your experience today.

Eighth Ray Meditation: GAINING CLARITY
INSIGHTS

Insights: list as many as you can remember.

_____

_____

_____

_____

Main concepts: what is the subject matter behind the concepts?

_____

_____

_____

_____

Meaning for you: how do you interpret these insights?

_____

_____

_____

_____

How can you use this in your daily life?

_____

_____

_____

_____

Why is that helpful?

_____

_____

_____

_____

Summary and Key Concepts

- The Eighth Ray is the Cleansing Ray. It is often used with the Seventh Ray.
- The Body of Light is that experience of self you use when you leave the Earth plane.
- The Spiritual Microtron is the smallest unit of energy. It is the spiritualization of matter and has its own consciousness.
- You can also use the Eighth Ray to bring clarity through your third eye, which is your sixth chakra.
- Call in the energy of the Eighth Ray when you feel your personal energy to be low. Allow it to invigorate you and refresh your energy.

Learnings

- Some life events are hard to understand, especially when they are filled with emotions. Use the energy of this Eighth Ray to help you move beyond these types of events and see how they prepare the way for new opportunities. This Ray offers clarity about how one event leads to another.

CHAPTER 15

The Ninth Ray

We use the Ninth Ray to remember and deepen our connections with our soul-level consciousness. A key aspect of being able to do this has to do with releasing old ties with the physical plane.

We have already discussed the notion of consciousness in relation to the Spiritual Microtron. Here we need to consider our own personal levels of consciousness. As multidimensional beings, we exist in multiple dimensions, each of which has unique characteristics of being. We are, of course, most familiar with this dimension and this level of consciousness. But even at this level of consciousness, there is personal consciousness that most of us are unaware of.

Let's start with our physical bodies. Our bodies consist of about 50 trillion cells. Each one of those cells has consciousness. Think about it. Millions of cells are replaced every day. How does a cell know when to reproduce? How does a cell know what its job is? How does one cell know to carry oxygen through the body? How does a different cell know to attack invading bacteria? Each cell has a consciousness that is passed on from one generation to the next. And these cells form together with common purpose to create bones, muscles, tissues, organs, and so on. Then these parts form together to create systems, like your endocrine system, your nervous system, your circulatory system, and so on. At each level of organization, there is consciousness. All of these levels of consciousness come together to create a whole-body consciousness.

As we move beyond the body, there are continuing levels of consciousness. We move to a level just above the body consciousness that I refer to as your inner wisdom. Some use the term "inner guidance." Then we come to the levels of your consciousness that are outside of this dimension. The next level is the Body of Light, which I have already briefly mentioned. Then beyond that is the soul-level consciousness, and beyond that is a level I call the higher self or whole self. And somewhere beyond that is your connection to the Creator or God.

The important thing to remember is that consciousness is a continuum. The labels I am using are simply arbitrary delineations along that continuum. So at the one end is the Spiritual Microtron, and at the other end is the Creator, and we exist at both ends and in between.

The reason that I went through this description of the levels of consciousness is so that I can help you narrow in on just what we are connecting to when we use the Ninth Ray. My belief is that you can actually communicate with all levels of consciousness. When we use the Ninth Ray, we are communicating with our consciousness somewhere above our Bodies of Light and somewhere below our higher self or whole self. This is where I believe our soul consciousness resides.

Another concept that is important to consider when discussing the Ninth Ray is the concept of personal identity, which is tied to consciousness. It is one thing to say I am a spiritual being having a physical experience. I am sure that most of us have heard that expression before. It is quite another to say that I am more than my experience in this lifetime. It is very different to identify not just with your physical self existing in this physical dimension but also with other expressions of yourself in totally different dimensions. When you shift your personal identity from that physical definition of yourself to a definition of yourself as living in multiple dimensions simultaneously, everything changes.

It becomes very difficult to continue playing small. It becomes very difficult for you to deny your role in creating your reality. It becomes very difficult to play the victim. You can continue to have all of those same experiences, but you now experience them as a matter of choice and personal expression. If you choose to move beyond your present limiting beliefs about who you are, you do that also as a matter of personal choice. You do it through personal empowerment.

Are you ready to see consciousness as a continuum? You don't have to agree with my arbitrary designations. Make up your own designations if that works for you. But seeing consciousness as a continuum is very helpful in working with these higher Rays.

Are you ready to define your personal identity as being more than just your physical self? If you are or if you already do, then we are ready to proceed. If you are not quite convinced, then let me suggest you continue on a bit more because a bigger picture is going to unfold, and perhaps a shift in perspective will help.

I started this section by stating that we use the Ninth Ray to connect with our soul-level consciousness. The Team has actually very little to say about the Ninth Ray. Here is their introduction.

> *The Ninth Ray is a luminescent, light blue-and-green blend of energy, and while the colors may not reflect the energy as you would imagine it to be, the energy that flows through this Ninth Ray is a blend of the First and Second Rays. The Ninth Ray is used to loosen the ties with the physical plane and establish contact with the soul level, the Christed part of self.*

We loosen our ties to the physical plane when we embrace the personal reality of our multidimensional existence. For some of us, however, these ties can be very strong. They are for me. I feel very comfortable in this physical dimension, and I enjoy the experience of being in this physical body. The Ninth Ray is very helpful in temporarily loosening our identification with our physical personalities. We are then free to journey out and establish that contact with our soul-level consciousness.

The Team used the expression "the Christed part of self," and there really is no further explanation given. I don't believe they make reference to "the Christed part of self" anywhere else in all the sessions. I am not going to attempt to define that expression here, but I think it would be helpful for you to have a clear understanding for yourself of the term "the Christ." I will say that as far as I know, it is a term of honor and reflects a degree of personal achievement. Keep in mind that they are making reference to a part of yourself.

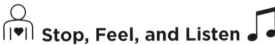 Stop, Feel, and Listen

Once again, take two minutes and feel the energy of this Ninth Ray. Read through this following passage and then put everything down and use your intention to bring in the Ninth Ray and establish that connection, even if it is brief, with your soul-level consciousness.

Begin by taking a gentle, relaxing breath. Allow your eyes to begin to gently close if you wish. See yourself in your sacred place, the place where you go that is beautiful and peaceful and perfectly safe. Now bring in the luminescent, light blue-and-green blend of energy that is the Ninth Ray and allow yourself to begin to float. And as you begin to float, you feel the ties to this Earth plane begin to loosen. And as they loosen even further, you feel yourself rising up. Allow yourself to rise up so much that you move beyond the clouds. Rise still further up until you see yourself in front of you as a being of beautiful, pure energy. Now allow yourself to connect with that image of your soul consciousness. Blend with it. Embrace it. And just relax and feel what that feels like. And when you have fully blended with your soul consciousness, anchor the memory into your physical consciousness. And when you have anchored that into your physical memory, begin to feel your consciousness returning to your body. Now take a gentle, deep breath and allow your consciousness to fully return to your physical body. And when you are ready, gently open your eyes and return to this place and this time.

Now write down below any insights that may have occurred to you while you were processing this information.

_____

_____

_____

_____

This experience of connecting with your soul-level consciousness is different than the next experience of connecting with your Body of Light. We do this experience first because it really is just remembering the connection for now. There will be much more about the soul-level consciousness when we discuss the Eleventh and Twelfth Rays. It is important to remember the connection here using the Ninth Ray because it helps us all to redefine our personal identities. It is important to move from an awareness of yourself as a multidimensional being to a knowing of yourself as being connected to all the levels of consciousness that we have discussed so far. This is why the Ninth Ray is so important.

Do not put too much pressure on yourself as you begin to use the Ninth Ray. You may not feel this blissful connection with all your levels of consciousness and all their connections with the dimensions in which they reside. There will come a time, hopefully, when you do feel those connections, but for now it is enough to remember that connection and to really feel it. Use the above short meditation as often as necessary to feel your connection to your soul-level consciousness deepen.

We also use the Ninth Ray to establish contact with the Body of Light. Here is the Team's description of that.

> _It may also be used to tune into what you would call the Body of Light, that experience of self that you will utilize when you leave the Earth plane. Use this Ray to tune into the Body of Light, to establish contact. When you meditate, bring in the Seventh Ray, the transmuting Ray. And then bring in the Eighth Ray and use it whatever way you wish. And bring in the Ninth Ray and use it with joy. Then call upon this Body of Light and dress yourself as if you are putting on new clothing. Establish contact with this new energy. Make its association, and having done that, you will be ready for the Tenth Ray._
>
> _As the collective you weaves this multidimensional tapestry and interconnects all levels of self, we give you this information about the Rays not to give you new limitations that you must incorporate, but to show you graphically the processes that are available._

I'd like to briefly mention the second paragraph above. Think of yourself as weaving a personal tapestry. This metaphor is one that the Team uses over and over again. You are weaving a personal tapestry in this lifetime that connects to all the other experiences you have had in this dimension. Then you connect it to all the other tapestries of all the other expressions of you in all the other dimensions. I think you will agree that this is one interesting tapestry.

The processes that they are graphically demonstrating are the individual suggestions the Team gives us for working with the Rays. These higher Rays build on each other, and as was suggested earlier, it is a good idea to work with them one at a time until all five of the higher Rays have been experienced. This is, collectively taken, a process of soul integration. I will have more to say about soul integration when we begin the in-depth discussion of the Tenth Ray.

Discussion

When we discuss the Ninth Ray, we are talking about establishing contact with two different levels of your consciousness. Remember the earlier discussion when I talked about individual consciousness as a continuum? One level that we use the Ninth Ray to establish contact with is the Body of Light. And the Team defines that level as "that experience of self that you will utilize when you leave the Earth plane." The other level of consciousness that we use the Ninth Ray to connect with is the soul level. Relatively speaking, this is a higher level of consciousness and one way to think about higher is this level resides in a higher dimension.

Another way of thinking about this is to remember that the Body of Light is connected to your current incarnation. Your soul-level consciousness is an assembly point, if you will, for all of your experiences in all the planes of manifestation. It has access to all of your experiences and many more experiences of aspects of itself that it has given birth to, although the term birth is probably misleading. It has understandably a much bigger perspective. The notion that I would like you to really get some clarity about from this discussion is that the Body of Light is, relatively speaking, nearby. It is just one dimension away. The soul-level consciousness is further away. How much further? I really don't know for sure, and I'm not sure it really makes all that much difference if it is two dimensions away or ten.

I have included two meditations that use the Ninth Ray. The first is the longer of the two, and with this meditation, we will connect with your soul-level consciousness. The second meditation will connect you with your Body of Light.

Ninth Ray Meditation: THE SOUL-LEVEL CONSCIOUSNESS

Arrange your feet either flat on the floor or comfortably tucked underneath you. Allow your hands to rest comfortably in your lap or at your sides, whichever feels more comfortable to you.

Let's begin with a gentle, deep breath. Focus your awareness on your relaxed breathing. Allow it to become nice and rhythmic. Keeping your awareness focused on your gentle, relaxed breathing, imagine that each time you breathe in, you breathe in a nice, fresh breath of relaxation. And with each exhale you breathe out stress. That's right—breathing in relaxation and releasing stress with each exhale.

Now I would like you to see your safe place, your sacred place. See that place you go to when you seek your safe, sacred place. It may be a place you have visited at one time or another. It may be a place you have seen on television or in the movies or in a magazine. Or it may be a place you have visited or imagined in the inner dimensions. Wherever it is, allow yourself to be there now and see yourself there. Very good. Feel how safe and protected you feel here. And invite in any guides or teachers that you might normally interact with here. Or perhaps you can just feel yourself surrounded by love. That's good.

Now I'd like for you to call in the Ninth Ray. Envision the luminous, light blue-and-green energy descending all around you. Now direct the Ninth Ray in front of you. Use it to begin to construct your bridge that you will cross over to establish contact with your soul-level consciousness. If for some reason a bridge is not suitable for you, feel free to use any other construct that will allow you to cross over and connect with your soul consciousness. Perhaps a staircase might work better. Use the Ninth Ray to build your bridge. See the construction taking place. You may choose to build a simple bridge made out of wood and stone, or you may prefer to build a glorious bridge made out of suspension cables. Or perhaps you would like to build a dazzling bridge made out of crystal energy. Construct any type of bridge you choose.

And when you have finished the construction of the bridge, I'd like you to begin to cross over the bridge. And when you get to the middle of the bridge, I'd like you to pause and take a step to the side and look underneath the bridge. What do you see underneath the bridge? Do you see water perhaps from a stream or a river? Maybe you see clouds or perhaps just stars? Whatever you see, notice whether what you are looking at is clear or cloudy. Notice if you can see anything in it or on it, and notice if it is flowing at all. And if it is flowing, is it flowing quickly or slowly? Just notice. Good.

Now continue to cross your bridge until you reach the other side. And on the other side you see a beautiful, crystal, white building. And in front of the building is a guide to greet you. And as you approach the guide, he or she motions you toward a doorway. You enter the beautiful, crystal, white building and inside waiting for you is your soul consciousness. Approach your soul consciousness and greet it. Relax yourself and begin to talk with your soul consciousness just like you would talk to a wonderful friend. Take some time to visit with your soul consciousness. I'll give you a minute or two.

(Wait no more than about three or four minutes.
If you are having trouble communicating with
your soul consciousness, allow your imagination

to open up and just imagine yourself talking
with your soul consciousness.)

In a minute we are going to begin our journey back. So take this remaining time to receive any information that your soul would like you to have before you depart.

(Wait one minute.)

Before we depart, take this remaining time to thank your soul-level consciousness for strengthening your connection today. Thank your soul consciousness for the loving communication you have shared today and know that you can bring back the entire memory of your meeting today with you. Pay attention to the response you receive. How does the response make you feel?

When you are ready, I'd like you to stand and exchange your final farewells with your soul consciousness, knowing that you are always connected and never alone. Now turn toward the door and begin to walk back outside, bringing with you all of the memories of today's meeting.

When you are outside again notice the guide and thank him or her for their help today. Then locate your bridge and begin to walk back across. And as you are walking back, when you reach the middle, I'd like you to stop once again and once again I'd like you to take a step to the side and look down under the bridge. I'd like you to focus on whatever is underneath the bridge and notice, just notice if there has been any change. Is it clear or cloudy under the bridge? Can you see anything in or on what is underneath the bridge? And is whatever is there moving or flowing? And if it is, is it moving or flowing quickly or slowly? Just notice.

And when you have noticed, I'd like you to continue your journey back across the bridge. And when you reach the other side, I'd like you to again see yourself in your safe, sacred place. And as you see yourself once again in your safe, sacred place, I'd like you to once again focus on your breathing. Now take a gentle, deep breath in and a gentle exhale out. And focusing on your breathing again, I'd like you to begin to allow your consciousness to return to your physical body. Gently move your fingers and your toes as you feel your consciousness slowly returning. Now allow your awareness to connect with your arms and your legs as your consciousness continues to return to your physical body. Take another gentle, deep breath. And when you are ready, gently and slowly open your eyes and return to this place and this time. Welcome back.

I suggest you take the time to complete the following worksheet. If you capture your insights now, right after you come back, they will still be fresh in your mind. You are likely to remember almost all of them.

Ninth Ray Meditation: THE SOUL-LEVEL CONSCIOUSNESS
INSIGHTS

Insights: list as many as you can remember.

Main concepts: what is the subject matter behind the concepts?

Meaning for you: how do you interpret these insights?

How can you use this in your daily life?

Why is that helpful?

This next meditation is shorter and involves establishing contact with the Body of Light. It was important to do, however, before we progress to the Tenth Ray. I mentioned earlier that we use the Ninth Ray to also establish contact with your Body of Light. In next chapter we will work with anchoring this energy into this dimension. Here we are simply going to make its acquaintance.

Ninth Ray Meditation: CONNECTING WITH THE BODY OF LIGHT

Let's begin by placing your feet firmly on the floor or by folding them underneath you if you prefer. Allow your hands to rest gently in your lap, or you may choose to hold them in a specific position. Now, take a gentle, deep breath and focus your awareness on your breath. Taking another deep, relaxing breath, become even more relaxed with each exhale. That's good.

Now I'd like you to envision your sacred place, that place where you go to connect with your inner wisdom, your higher consciousness. This can be a place you have visited in real life, or it can be a place you may have seen in the movies or on television or in a magazine. Or perhaps it is a place where you go in the inner realms. Choose whichever place is most suitable for your experience today of connecting with your Body of Light.

And when you have the best place for you to be today, I'd like you to bring in the Ninth Ray, the light blue-and-green colored Ray, which is the bridge to your Body of Light. Remember that we use the Ninth Ray to help us loosen ties with the physical world. So as you bring in this Ninth Ray, allow it to totally surround you. And as you feel this energy begin to lift your energetic level, feel yourself becoming lighter and lighter, feel your ties to this third dimension begin to loosen.

Now allow your consciousness to begin to separate from the image of your physical body. Allow it to slightly drift away and, as it does, look back and observe the image of your physical body here in your sacred place. And know that as you move to connect with your Body or Light, your physical body is safe and protected.

Now using the Ninth Ray, that beautiful, light blue-and-green energy, allow your consciousness to continue to rise up. You may see a bridge to cross over, or you may just see yourself floating among the stars, or use any other imagery that helps you to travel to meet your Body of Light. And as you feel yourself traveling, I'd like you to become aware of a beautiful, white, crystal house just off in the distance. And I'd like you to head now to this beautiful, shimmering house.

And see yourself in front of this magnificent structure now. And you notice a guide is standing in front, and the guide beckons you to enter by pointing to a doorway. You thank the guide for showing you the way, and you enter the house. And inside the house, you see your Body of Light. It is waiting for you. So now I would like you to walk up to your Body of Light and blend with it. And as you blend with it, allow yourself to release those limiting thoughts that you have about who you are. Release your limiting thoughts that you are just your physical body.

Embrace your energetic Body of Light. Feel the energy as you have never felt it before. This is a higher level of energy than your physical body, and with it comes a higher level of understanding. Allow yourself to connect with that higher level of understanding. Allow your mind to move beyond its current limits.

Now focus your attention on your heart center and allow your heart to open. Allow your heart to be free of the human experiences that have limited how much love it can express. Feel how safe it is to let your heart expand. What does it feel like to love so freely without any fear? Here in this higher realm, allow yourself to receive love like you have never received it before. Invite in the love that your higher consciousness has for you. Invite in the love that your Body of Light is always surrounded by.

Take a minute and allow yourself to adjust to all this new freedom.

(Wait one minute.)

In a moment—not now but in a moment—we will begin our journey back. So take this time to receive any final insights or gifts that your Body of Light has for you.

(Wait one minute.)

Now we will begin our journey back. Thank your Body of Light for allowing you to connect with it today in such a loving way. Exchange your farewells, and when you are ready, turn and locate the door. Step outside, and when you do you once again see the guide outside. Thank the guide for showing you the way to where your Body of Light was waiting for you.

Continue to return to your sacred place. Whatever means you used to get here, use the same way to return to your sacred place. And as you return to your sacred place, bring back with you the entire memory of this experience. Bring back the memory of how it feels to blend with your Body of Light. Bring back that feeling of love. Allow that feeling of love to surround your physical body.

Now as you begin to focus on your physical body again, take a deep, gentle breath and feel the air entering into your lungs. And gently exhale establishing a gentle, rhythmic breathing pattern. And as you focus on your breath, gently move your fingers and your toes. And as you move your fingers and your toes, allow your consciousness to begin to return to your physical body. Now focus on your arms and your legs, allowing your consciousness to fully return to your physical body. And when you are ready, gently and slowly open your eyes and return to this place and this time. Welcome back.

Again, I recommend that you record your insights and experiences on the worksheet. Capturing this information right away can be very helpful.

Ninth Ray Meditation: CONNECTING WITH THE BODY OF LIGHT
INSIGHTS

Insights: list as many as you can remember.

....

....

....

....

Main concepts: what is the subject matter behind the concepts?

....

....

....

....

Meaning for you: how do you interpret these insights?

....

....

....

....

How can you use this in your daily life?

....

....

....

....

Why is that helpful?

....

....

....

....

This experience can show you another aspect of your multidimensional selves that you were probably unaware of. It is important to experience this aspect of yourself and integrate it into your awareness before you attempt to bring it down and anchor it into this dimension. It is important to process these two steps individually. I had months to process and integrate this information back when we first received it. I really feel this needs to be done before you can move on to the most important part of the Ninth and Tenth Rays—the anchoring of the Body of Light.

Summary and Key Concepts

- Our bodies, which contain over 50 trillion cells and can rightly be considered as universes in themselves, have multiple levels of consciousness.
- Consciousness is a continuum.
- We are multidimensional beings with simultaneous existences in multiple dimensions.
- We have multiple expressions of personal consciousness within the same dimension.
- We use the Ninth Ray to remember our connections to our Bodies of Light, which are just one of our simultaneous expressions of self.

Learnings

- While it is true that we exist simultaneously in multiple dimensions, this current existence is most relevant for us.
- We have never been disconnected from our soul-level consciousness. Most of us, however, have forgotten that connection. When we forget the connection, we allow ourselves the illusion of being stand-alone individuals disconnected from All That Is. There is purpose in creating this illusion.
- We integrate our experiences in consciousness into our personal tapestries. Imagine your integrated self as more beautiful than the tapestries that used to hang on castle walls in medieval Europe.

CHAPTER 16

Checking Progress

This entire journey we are on together is about raising up your personal energetic level to a point where the energy of the Body of Light can be anchored into the physical body. In order to be successful with the next part of the process, the anchoring in of the Body of Light, a certain level of effort is needed to release the lower-level energies that hold us back. At the same time, new concepts need to be assimilated and integrated to help us develop a new understanding of ourselves.

Julie and I are familiar with the process of integrating the messages that the Team shares with us. They confronted us in one session—actually they confronted me—and asked if we had done our work. I am sure it goes without saying that they wouldn't have asked us about it if it were not true. Here are their comments.

You have invited us to be with you and we ask, "How much have you studied? How much have you integrated?" The words that we speak with you float by, and until you grasp them and draw them into that which you are, they are lost; they are without depth and dimension, without a place to call home. They are a thought floating in the ether waiting to be discovered, waiting to be realized, to be acted upon.

You wish to know of the Twelve Rays, yet you have not integrated our messages. You wish to know of the new energies, the light substance floating into the universal sea of electronic light. Are you ready to learn, to reawaken the energies, to know how they move?

Have you truly discussed them, or have you looked at the words only? Have you combined the messages?

Have you discussed what works for you? What is your truth? We give you concepts—broad and encompassing. We ask you to think. We ask you to feel what really is right for you. IT IS NOT OUR PLACE TO GROW FOR YOU. Your growth through the interaction to your being, to the concepts we present, is what we are waiting to observe.

You will find as we progress, you will have questions with some of the material and some of [the] concepts that we give. You have questions, and this is good, for we … we desire that you are your teacher, not I. Do not take what we give and never question. Question it all. Press us. Ask us to elaborate. Question again until you have formed your own thoughts and concepts. This is a Master. We know no more than you; we simply see clearer because of our place.

I can still remember how I felt during this session. I was looking for a place to hide. I couldn't refute anything they were saying. There was no defense. I was indeed not doing the work. They called me on it, and they were right. How did I think any of this was going to make a difference if I did not integrate it?

I was so comfortable in receiving the information and filing it away in the "oh, that is interesting" folder. I knew where it was filed and could bring it out when I needed it. Hopefully, I would still remember where to find it. But more than likely, I would have gone on to something else, another book or a new topic from the Team, and what I received that day would be long forgotten.

They were right, and it was time to make a choice. Did I really want to own this wisdom? Did I really want to integrate it into my being? Or was it quite all right to just file it away and keep moving forward? I was being offered this extraordinary opportunity to dialogue directly with beings from beyond our dimension. Was I ready to really take advantage of it? I can honestly say that it felt pretty overwhelming at the time.

I was so embarrassed during this session. I knew they were right. I felt I had just received the information and filed it away. But this wasn't like reading just another book on spiritual enlightenment. This was one-on-one instruction on the workings of the universe and beyond. Yes, it was exciting to be communicating with the Team in this manner. Who would believe that I was doing this?

They knew I needed a different level of engagement with this new information. They knew I needed a different level of commitment in order to integrate the information and use it for my own personal growth. They called me out and asked me to choose. How did I want to value their help and assistance? The answer was simple of course. I wanted to continue with the sessions, and I wanted to know more. And I knew that in order for that to happen, I had to participate in the effort at a higher level. I needed to process and integrate and decide what fit and what didn't.

I ask the same of you. You can continue on, read the remaining pages of this book, and neatly file it away in your "oh, that is interesting" folder, or you can do the work and integrate the energies that I have presented up until now. It is your choice, and of course, I will not be confronting you like the Team confronted us.

I will just point out that the benefit from working with the Rays is yours. Find your level of comfort with them. Whatever you choose will impact the rest of your experience with the remainder of this book.

Remember that you can always choose again if you find your original choice did not bring you what you feel is right for you. I am just trying to make a point here that your experience of the Tenth Ray will vary based on how much effort you have put into working with the material presented so far. But that is really true about most everything, isn't it? Our experience of what we perceive as reality is always shaped by our understanding and our beliefs.

CHAPTER 17

The Tenth Ray

The Tenth Ray is the Body of Light. The Team has defined the Body of Light previously as "that experience of self that you will utilize when you leave the Earth plane." It is time now to look more closely at the Tenth Ray. Here is the Team's introduction to the Tenth Ray.

The Tenth Ray, as you may have already studied, is a pearl-colored luminescent energy and consists of the First, the Second, and the Third Rays, with the white light of wholeness added. It can actually, if you let it, code the Body of Light into the physical structure. It is the Body of Light.

This Tenth Ray can enable you to lock in those changes you are seeking to make, whatever they are. And that's important, for you are all undergoing this process now on Earth. There are large quantities of this energy available, and if you recognize its presence through your own evolutionary point, you will be getting in touch with it and have access to it. All others do not even know it is here. So if you are sensitive to this energy, you see then that there are great changes going on within self.

The intensity of this Ray provides an opportunity to learn in the polarity areas because, of course, when fully realized, the Tenth Ray allows the oneness of self to be experienced, the complete balance of the male and female aspects.

This opportunity of the Tenth Ray is to perceive the Body of Light while in a physical structure. You always have it; it has been and will always be with you, but you have yet to realize it.

All the higher Rays are blends of the lower Rays. The Tenth is a blend of the first three Rays with "the white light of wholeness added." I don't have a good definition of the white light of wholeness. Most of us have experienced it, and it is perhaps best for each one to define it based upon our own personal experiences.

The Body of Light

Let's consider the significance of the Tenth Ray. It can code, or anchor, the Body of Light into our physical structure, our bodies. Why is this important? It seems this is the significant change, the huge opportunity available now for humankind that the Team keeps talking to us about. We can begin the process of raising the energetic level of this entire physical dimension by raising our own energetic levels. The Earth will follow us in raising its energetic levels.

Why would we want to raise the energetic levels of this dimension? To allow for more choice, and more choice allows for more and varied experiences. The opportunity exists now to move from a reality where spiritual progress has mainly come about through pain and suffering to a reality of experiencing spiritual progress and growth through grace and ease. How do you feel about that? Are you ready for something different?

What we are really talking about here is the advancement of life on this planet. And we are talking about all life, not just human life. We are the creators of this shift. It is up to us to make it happen. We have been given the tools to assist us in moving forward. All we have to do is use them. What a wonderful time to be living on the planet. We have the opportunity to participate in this monumental shift. It is starting with all of us.

The Team talks about the changes that are going on now. They are not only talking about the personal changes that we all are experiencing, but also the sweeping shifts occurring all over the planet. There is a great surge in personal empowerment. The access to electronic information is allowing people to understand that life is not the same everywhere, and there is no reason at all for poverty, disease, starvation, or war. People everywhere are empowering themselves, and as they do, the institutions of repression, control, and scarcity are crumbling. I think we all feel the shifts.

The Team further explains that we can use the Tenth Ray to experience the oneness of self. We can experience the "complete balance of the male and the female aspects."

I do not think it is reasonable to expect this complete balance to occur overnight. We are, however, laying the foundation for this experience. Just imagine what it will be like to have the complete balance of male and female within the same consciousness. Makes you wonder, doesn't it?

What about this Body of Light that we have yet to realize? According to the Team, we have always had it, and most of us are unaware of it. So why now? Why are we being made aware of it now?

The Body of Light that we speak of is not the energy body or the etheric body as you know it. It is a higher vibration. You must really change your vibration in order to bring it into physical existence. After the soul merge, which in a sense recodes the physical cells, this becomes a model for physical cells and has never been possible before in human existence. It is a doorway to what you are seeking. It is the Body of Light.

Anchoring the Body of Light into the physical body is a key component of the soul merge. The soul merge as I understand it is bringing more of your soul-level consciousness into this physical dimension. The Body of Light is a part of that soul-level consciousness that has never been brought into this dimension before. Using the Ninth Ray to establish contact with the soul-level consciousness is another aspect of the soul merge. This is an ongoing process not just for individuals but for humankind in general.

All of this raising up of personal energy is also part of the process. When you put it all together, the effect is that our individual cells begin to reproduce themselves at this higher level, a level that has never before been possible. That sounds pretty exciting to me.

 Stop, Feel, and Listen ♫

Take two minutes now to acquaint yourself with this beautiful energy. Read the following passage and, when you are done, put everything down and just follow along.

Allow your eyes to gently and slowly close. See or visualize the beautiful, luminescent, pearl-colored energy of the Tenth Ray. Focus your attention and direct a column of pearlescent energy to descend upon you from above. Feel its intensity. Connect with its electrical qualities. These are the pastel blue and pink flickers of the Spiritual Microtron. Send it through you into the Earth. In this way you draw it closer into your reality and into the Earth's reality. Bring it into your body. Allow each and every one of your 50 trillion cells to connect with it. Begin the process of anchoring the Body of Light into your physical body by having each cell connect with this beautiful energy of the Tenth Ray. Relax and feel it move through you. And when you are ready, take a gentle, deep breath and slowly open your eyes. Return to this place and this time.

Now to really get value from this short exercise, write down any insights that may have occurred to you while you were processing this information.

I hope you enjoyed that brief introduction. These stop-and-feel interludes are meant to be just brief introductions to each of the Rays. I hope you have taken the time. It really is just a couple of minutes to experience the Rays this way. I just want to reiterate a point that the Team made earlier. When we work with these higher Rays, there is a cumulative effect. Each Ray needs to be felt and integrated before going on and working with the next one.

The Spiritual Microtron

Now let's discuss the Spiritual Microtron in greater detail. As best as I can understand it, the Spiritual Microtron is the smallest particle of energy that all of creation is comprised of. Before it manifests as matter, it is pure energy, and this energy is imbued with consciousness and intelligence. Here is the Team's first explanation of the Spiritual Microtron.

> For intelligence to act, there must be intelligence to be acted upon, and the divine substance records almost like a photographic film whatever quality the individual invokes through his thought, feeling, and spoken word. Intelligence is omnipresent, forever present. It is in the electronic light and is now present in physicality with the Microtron.
>
> Light is the center point of life or energy within every atom and is the substance for all physical manifestation. We speak of the atom here because the lower rate of vibration composing physicality is the atomic structure we are trying to perfect. When you envelop or focus upon a person, place, thing, or condition within the white light of the Source, you penetrate through the atomic structure into the electronic, wherein there is no physical imperfection.
>
> In the use of the Spiritual Microtron, one penetrates the structure of relative imperfection, and then whatever the intention is focused upon can be brought forth as perfect. It is not just perfection as the Creator sees it; it is the Creator's perfection expressed.

This particular passage is a little more complex than most of their discussions. I summarize most of the above into the concept that everything is composed of the Spiritual Microtron. We can direct this energy through focused attention to manifest whatever we choose in this physical dimension. It is really from this understanding of the makeup of matter that we can conclude that everything has consciousness. It may not seem to be the case, but it is nonetheless.

Everything has consciousness. Everything doesn't have human consciousness of course. That is reserved for us humans, but it is consciousness nonetheless. We can say that a rock or a chair has consciousness, and most people would ask how that is possible. The answer is simple. They have rock consciousness, or they have chair consciousness, and it is as difficult for us to perceive rock consciousness as it is for the rock to perceive human consciousness. Consciousness all comes from the same place. It comes from the Creator and moves into our dimension through the Spiritual Microtron.

The phrase, "For intelligence to act, there must be intelligence to be acted upon," is one of my most favorite from all the sessions. In a nutshell, it describes how things are manifested in the physical dimension. We possess the intelligence to create. But it only happens if there is intelligence on the other end that perceives our intentions. And when we clearly communicate our intentions, through focused attention, we become the conscious creators of our world.

The Spiritual Microtron has a specific connection to the Tenth Ray.

> We have talked in the past about the Spiritual Microtron and briefly touched on what it is. And if you were perceptive, you may have already realized the link between the Spiritual Microtron and the light body, the Body of Light that we have talked about, for this energy is one and the same. This finely tuned, higher vibration comes to you and is anchored in your dimension through the Tenth Ray.
>
> It is the spiritualization of matter. The material is manifestation of spirit, the blending of which you create in harmony with the Creator, and it comes through as a fine, soft, yet powerful energy when you have risen in your own vibration, when you have released, released yourself from the lower vibrations of emotion, when you have centered yourself within your heart, when you have disciplined yourself away from your limits, when you have surrendered to a reality beyond the restrictions in your dimension.

Perhaps you can see how the prior Rays and your utilization of them have prepared you for this process, this process of working with the Body of Light and the Spiritual Microtron? The Team is mentioning all of those processes that we have discussed before, the lifting or cleansing of the lower vibrational energy, the releasing of personal limits, and the redefinition of our personal identities not based on our physical selves but expanded to include the reality of our multidimensional existence.

Take a moment and contemplate the phrase "the spiritualization of matter." Everything that you see in this dimension is the manifestation of Spirit, the manifestation of the Source, or as some would say, the manifestation of God. I don't use the word God often mainly because of the many and varied definitions of the word. I do feel it is appropriate here because no matter what definition of God is used, few organized religions would argue with the notion that all of creation is a manifestation of God. That is my understanding of what the Team is telling us about the Spiritual Microtron. It is the energy that comes directly from the Source, and it contains the imprint of the Source within it.

Here is a further comment from the Team about the nature of the Spiritual Microtron.

The Tenth Ray is a pearlized energy. Within this vibration exists the Spiritual Microtron, the Body of Light, and in your world, there are limits to what you can visualize because of your environment. But we tell you within this energy there exists the softest pastels of blue and pink, and they are alive, as alive as you.

The Spiritual Microtron has both intelligence and consciousness, and those aspects alone are a good working definition of what constitutes life. Remember that this energy is directed by focused intention and creates the manifested universe that we perceive as our own. It can be shaped and formed and directed to create anything we choose as long as it is within the guidelines of our physical laws. I hope you can see why this concept is so important for us to comprehend and why the Team has spent so much time explaining it to us.

 Discussion

I touched on the Tenth Ray a little in previous chapters. I have also talked a little about the Body of Light and the Spiritual Microtron. Now is the time to bring it all together for you. I am talking about progress. I want to talk about moving forward in your personal development as both an individual and as a member of humankind.

When you have fully anchored the Body of Light, you will have fully opened that channel to Spirit. You will be open to the notion of Spirit's existence and allow that energy of higher self to move into your consciousness. As you work with the exercises that we have given you, you will be able to draw that Body of Light into your physical being through the intention of doing this. Simply invite it in. It's very simple. And open yourself, which can be more challenging. So many invite and then slam the door. They want and don't want. They pretend. They say look what I'm doing. It's all a façade.

This next text was received in April 2010. They mention the Council of Twelve, and there is really no explanation of just who they are. I assume it is not really all that important for us to know who the Council of Twelve is.

The Tenth Ray has never been applied or implemented in any universe the way it is in your universe now! What do we mean by this? We mean that all Twelve Rays have been functioning at the universal level forever, but their application was to balance creation with whatever level of these higher Rays could be interpreted and used to support in harmony physical creation.

The Rays step down from the less dense dimensions to the next level of creation the amount of energy that respective levels can handle. What the expanded Source has mandated is a stepping down from our level of spiritual energy, which means energy without atoms. The significance of this is very profound, meaning that the fourth through the sixth dimensions now can also assimilate the non-atomic material, which we're calling the Microtron and which is of such a fine vibrational frequency that your most sophisticated scientific equipment has not yet discovered spiritual energy.

This spiritual energy, the Microtron, is stepped down from the levels associated with the universal Council of Twelve through an elaborate electromagnetic grid system established by the archangels for the spiritual benefit of all of creation, but particularly your fourth through sixth densities. Thus, the emphasis now on the spiritualization of matter through the Tenth Ray! It is very significant at this point in time that the co-creators here in physicality begin to integrate the Tenth Ray in a gentle and correct manner.

We wish to remind you that the basic principle of healing on this planet through mass consciousness is neither light nor dark. It is simply what the total of you, the creator of your own reality, have allowed.

Remember back to the last meditations with the Ninth Ray. You connected with your soul-level consciousness. I invited you to do a second meditation using the Ninth Ray to establish contact with your Body of Light. In our discussion of consciousness, I talked about consciousness as being a continuum. The soul consciousness exists in a higher dimension than the Body of Light, relatively speaking. When we bring in the Body of Light to this dimension, we also bring in the awareness of the soul consciousness. I hope that makes sense to you.

In this chapter you are going to begin to anchor your Body of Light into this dimension. That is what you are going to do in the next meditation. Before you do that, let me comment on the last part of what you just read.

The Team mentions the Council of Twelve, and to the best of my recollection, this is the only time they mentioned the council. They don't generally speak about the hierarchy that is found in the higher dimensions. They keep it simple on purpose. It seems to me that they provided this level of detail here because it is a big deal. They are really emphasizing the uniqueness of what is happening now in our evolution. They say, "The Tenth Ray has never been applied or implemented in any universe the way it is in your universe now!" That sounds like a big deal to me. They further go on to explain that what is different is the stepping down of the Spiritual Microtron into our fourth dimension. It hasn't been available in our dimension until now. They again used the phrase "the spiritualization of matter."

They reminded us that we are co-creators of this reality, and the time has come to step up to our responsibility and use the abilities that we have in "a gentle and correct manner." So this is a very special time, and you and I are here to experience it, and we are here for a reason. As you do this work using these higher

Rays, keep in mind that something very special is going on here, and we are all a part of it. It is just that some are more aware of it than others, and of course, that is the way it needs to be.

This next meditation, as I mentioned earlier, allows you to connect with your Body of Light and anchor it into your physical body in this dimension. This is truly groundbreaking.

 ## Tenth Ray Meditation: ANCHORING THE BODY OF LIGHT

Begin by getting yourself comfortably seated. Allow your hands to relax comfortably in your lap or at your sides. Have your feet comfortably on the floor or any other way that you find comfortable. Take a gentle, deep breath. As you exhale, allow any stress or anxiety to flow out. Focus now on your breathing and continue gentle, relaxed breathing—breathing in deep relaxation and breathing out any stress or tension that you may still feel. That's good.

Now I'd like you to select a beautiful, relaxing, safe place in your mind. This may be a place you have actually been to before, or it may be a place you have just seen on television, in a movie, or perhaps in a magazine. Or it may be a place you have only dreamt about or perhaps a place in the inner dimensions that you have visited before. This is your safe place, your sacred place.

And once you have selected this place, the place that is most appropriate for you today, I'd like for you to see yourself there. Be there now. And when you see yourself there, I'd like you to begin to look around and notice all the lush, beautiful scenery that there is. Look around now at the flowers and the bushes and the trees. Perhaps you can see hills or mountains in the distance. Or perhaps there is water, perhaps a lake or a pond, or maybe a beach nearby. Now look up into the sky and see if there are beautiful, white fluffy clouds in the air. See how blue the sky appears. Perhaps you can see birds flying?

Now listen. What can you hear? Can you hear the song of the birds? Can you hear the wind in the bushes and the trees? Can you hear the sound of the water? Perhaps there are waves breaking on the beach? What else can you hear?

Now looking at the beauty of this, your sacred place, your safe place, listen to all the gentle sounds of this place. I'd like you to take a moment and feel how good it feels to be here. Feel how calm and relaxed you are right now.

Now I'd like you to bring in the blue and green energy of the Ninth Ray and allow it to move right through you and flow down into Mother Earth. And as the energy of the Ninth Ray moves through you, I'd like you to feel your energy levels rising. Feeling your energy levels rising, I'd like you to imagine yourself rising up, rising up to connect once again with your Body of Light. That's right—allow that image of your Body of Light to grow stronger. And now, allow your consciousness to reach out to your Body of Light and make contact with it. And allow that connection to your Body of Light to grow stronger.

Now I invite you to direct the energy of your Body of Light, the luminous, pearlescent energy of the Tenth Ray. I invite you to direct that energy down into your physical body. Allow it to begin to enter your physical body. Allow it to move into your body. You may choose to bring it into your body from above, allowing it to move down through your head, into your shoulders, down through your abdomen, into your hips, and down through your legs. Or you may choose to let it surround you and bring it into your body from all sides simultaneously.

Direct the energy of the Tenth Ray—the luminous, pearlescent energy— to move into all parts of your body, to each and every cell of your body. And now I'd like you to envision one individual cell in your body. Your body contains around 50 trillion cells, so pick a particular cell. It may be a heart cell or perhaps a brain cell or maybe a blood cell or even maybe a muscle cell. Pick one cell and allow that image of that cell to grow stronger in your mind. And when that image of your cell is clear in your mind, I'd like you to imagine you can talk to it. And imagining you can talk to this cell, I'd like you to ask it if it feels the energy of the Tenth Ray. And if it feels the energy, I'd like you to ask it how the energy feels. What effect is the energy having on it? Take a minute or two and have this conversation with your cell now.

(Wait one minute.)

Now in a minute, I'm going to ask you to communicate with another part of your body. So take this remaining time to finish this conversation with your cell.

(Wait one minute.)

Now I would like you to choose an organ of your body. It may be your heart, your lungs, a kidney, your spleen, or any organ that you choose. Remember that your brain is also an organ. Or you may choose a gland in your body. And when you have chosen, I'd like you to again imagine you can talk to this body part. I'd like you to ask it if it feels the energy of the Tenth Ray. And if it feels the energy, I'd like you to ask it how the energy feels. What is its sense of the energy? What effect is the energy having on it? Take a minute or two and have this conversation with your body part now.

(Wait two minutes.)

In a minute I'm going to ask you to communicate with another part of your body. So take this remaining time to finish this conversation with your body part.

(Wait one minute.)

Now I would like you to connect with the consciousness of your body. I'd like you to again imagine you can talk to your body consciousness. I'd like you to ask it if it feels the energy of the Tenth Ray. And if it feels the energy, I'd like you to ask it how the energy feels. What is its sense of the energy? What effect is the energy having on it? Take a minute or two and have this conversation with your body consciousness now.

(Wait two minutes.)

In a minute, I'm going to ask you to communicate with your inner wisdom. So take this remaining time to finish this conversation with your body consciousness.

(Wait one minute.)

Now I would like you to connect with your inner wisdom, your inner guidance. And having connected with your inner wisdom, I'd like you to ask it its perception of how the energy of the Tenth Ray is affecting your body. Take a minute or two and have this conversation with your inner wisdom now.

(Wait two minutes.)

In a minute, I'm going to ask you to remember this conversation with each of your body parts. So take this remaining time to finish this conversation with your inner wisdom.

(Wait one minute.)

And now I'd like you to see the parts of your consciousness you connected with today all together in front of you. See your cell, your body organ or gland, your body consciousness, and your inner wisdom, and notice the connection that you have with each part. And notice how each part is connected to each other part. Take a minute and feel all these connections.

(Wait one minute.)

Now take a minute and feel your connection to the Spiritual Microtron.

Feel your connection to your soul-level consciousness. Feel your connection to your higher self. And feel your connection to the Source, to the Creator, to All That Is. Take a minute and feel all these connections.

(Wait one minute.)

Remember that you are a constant projection of your higher self. There is no need to search for that connection. You do not have to struggle to find it. You are always connected. All you need to do is let go of any beliefs that you are alone, that you are not connected.

In a minute, we will begin our journey back to the physical realm. But for right now, I'd like you to know that you can remember and bring back with you all the memories of everything you experienced today while working with the Tenth Ray and anchoring the energy of your Body of Light into your physical body. Or you may choose to only remember certain portions of your experience. It is all up to you.

Now as you begin to return to the physical realm, I'd like you to take a gentle, deep breath. And as you begin this gentle, rhythmic breathing, I'd like you to begin to allow your consciousness to return to your physical body. And as you allow your consciousness to begin to return, I'd like you to gently begin to move your fingers and your toes. And now continue to breathe nicely and gently and connect once again with your arms and your legs. And as you are connecting again with your arms and your legs, allow your consciousness to fully return to your physical body. And when you are ready, gently open your eyes and return to this place and this time. Welcome back.

Again, please take the time to record your experience on the following worksheet.

Tenth Ray Meditation: ANCHORING THE BODY OF LIGHT
INSIGHTS

Insights: list as many as you can remember.

_____

_____

_____

_____

Main concepts: what is the subject matter behind the concepts?

_____

_____

_____

_____

Meaning for you: how do you interpret these insights?

_____

_____

_____

_____

How can you use this in your daily life?

_____

_____

_____

_____

Why is that helpful?

_____

_____

_____

_____

I hope your experience of this meditation was very meaningful. This is what we have been working toward, this experience of the Body of Light in this dimension. I highly recommend that you repeat this meditation as often as you like. You can even omit certain parts of it if you do not have enough time to do the entire meditation. For example, you don't have to connect with all the body parts. You could choose to just connect with one particular body part each time you do it. You might also choose not to connect with any body parts and instead just feel the energy of the Tenth Ray move through your physical body. There are many possible variations, and of course, you are encouraged to create personal journeys on your own.

As you begin this anchoring of the Body of Light into your physical body, be aware of any shifts you may be experiencing that might correspond with this new, higher, energetic level. This could be anything from what used to set you off in the past—perhaps a coworker or a mother-in-law or whatever—to shifts in food cravings away from highly processed foods to more natural foods. There could be all types of changes, some very subtle and some very overt. You may just find yourself thinking one day, "Hmm … I don't do that anymore," or "I don't crave that anymore." Just be on the lookout.

As a way to sum up all of this section on Rays Eight through Ten, I'd like to share with you a personal journey that comes directly from the Team. I'm going to include it here, and I'm going to try to keep it as near to the way they delivered it.

 Tenth Ray Meditation: COMBINATION

You will see that this was intended for Julie and me, so just imagine they are talking to you directly. You can use your own guides and teachers if you like—your own team—or you can feel free to invite our Team to work with you. Choose whatever you like. The Merkaba Valley, just to refresh your memory, is a valley with six peaks that overlook it. So just imagine one energetic being on each of the peaks.

> *And now we come to walk you actively through an exercise for you to use to gently allow these energies, the higher Rays, to work their way through all parts of your being.*
>
> *So now, we invite you, as you have invited us, to imagine you are sitting within the Merkaba Valley. You are sitting in the center, and on each peak, we join you. And as you place us one at a time, as you invite us to sit with you on each point, see that we are holding a Violet Flame, a point of light on each peak, and surrender. We surrender to you our wisdom and our guidance, our love. And when you have placed each of us, when you have acknowledged each of us, then acknowledge yourself, the one that is with you and see that you hold the Violet Flame. As you are holding each hand, see the Violet Flame rise up. Feel the energy move*

through your essence. Feel the energy permeate through the Merkaba until we are all encompassed with one beautiful Violet Flame. You have opened and allowed your team and yourself to sit as one, to share, to integrate. Feel this energy flow through your physical bodies.

In your mind's eye, see this violet energy flow through. Feel it as it swirls around your physical body. And now visualize the Eighth Ray moving through. Visualize each of us on these points of light, modifying our colors, our vibrations, and notice the flame as you sit in the center and how it begins to modify, change, how with violet becomes mixed with the green. And ever so slowly, the air becomes lighter, the violet more pure. This is the wholeness of Source. And now this violet begins to fade as the Ninth Ray moves in and the green remains.

The violet takes on a pastel blue, a higher, softer, vibratory, luminescent color. And we—as the points of light—begin to glow, and you feel this as a white light, and it moves. It fills this Merkaba, and you surrender to it. And as you allow this energy to draw closer and closer to the center, into where you are, as you open up to it, it changes again. And it becomes the Tenth Ray, and it swirls through you, moves around you. It sparkles. It's alive. It carries with it an intelligence, a wisdom, that is available to all that open to it. And if you can [see], mixed in this pearlized, luminescent energy, is this pale baby blue, a beautiful pastel, and a beautiful pastel pink. These are the energies of the Spiritual Microtron. And as they pass through you, feel their energy as they connect with each and every cell of your body.

The Tenth Ray is a pearlized energy. Within this vibration exists the Spiritual Microtron, the Body of Light. And in your world, there are limits to what you can visualize because of your environment. But we tell you within this energy there exists the softest pastels of blue and pink, and they are alive, as alive as you. Allow them to move through you, to help raise your energetic level, to help anchor in this Body of Light.

And now become aware of your surroundings once again. Remember this experience of the Tenth Ray and use this exercise to strengthen your connection to your Body of Light.

Please take the time to write down your experiences on the following worksheet.

Tenth Ray Meditation: COMBINATION
INSIGHTS

Insights: list as many as you can remember.

Main concepts: what is the subject matter behind the concepts?

Meaning for you: how do you interpret these insights?

How can you use this in your daily life?

Why is that helpful?

I hope you found this exercise that comes directly from our Team useful. It is a very powerful, short journey through Rays Seven to Ten, and hopefully, you can feel the energy as it moves through you. As each Ray shifts into the next, the texture of the energy changes. I hope you can feel how each Ray is different yet builds from the preceding Ray. The Team suggests we use this technique to gently allow the energy of these Rays to move through your entire being. Never be afraid of directing the energy of the Rays. Use them with focused attention, but use them with respect, for they come to us directly from the Source, and we should always treat them as gifts given especially for us. They are here for our use in this physical dimension. And they have never been available to us before like they are now!

The higher Rays are all about soul integration. I hope you take some time and really work with these energies and concepts. This understanding of yourself as a multidimensional being is the key concept to be developed and embraced in this section. I have provided meditations to help you experience the energies of the higher Rays, but these Rays themselves are not the destination. They are only the tools to achieve the desired outcome.

I hope you can take the time to master the tools and that through your mastery of the Rays, you will realize a new and different definition of self. Hopefully, you will see yourself differently, and this is very important because this new definition of self enables you to open the doorway to Rays Eleven and Twelve. The Twelfth Ray is the New Awareness, and the New Awareness starts with your new perception of your personal reality.

Summary and Key Concepts

- The Tenth Ray is the Body of Light. It is a pearlized energy.
- The Tenth Ray has never been applied or implemented in any universe the way it is in our universe now.
- The anchoring of the Body of Light has never before been possible in human existence.
- The Spiritual Microtron is the spiritualization of matter.
- Within the energy of the Tenth Ray exists the softest pastels of blue and pink (the Spiritual Microtron), and they are alive, as alive as you.

Learnings

- Anchoring the Body of Light into the physical body brings more of your soul-level consciousness into this physical dimension.
- When you have fully anchored the Body of Light, you will have fully opened that channel to Spirit. You will be open to the notion of Spirit's existence and allow the energy of higher self to move into your consciousness.
- This is a unique opportunity for all humankind.

CHAPTER 18

Let's Review

I have been guiding you through a process—a process Julie and I went through together—that requires time to integrate. How much time does it take to integrate? I can't answer that for you, but I'm pretty sure it can be done faster now than when we did it. The energies are different now, and I believe the motivation level for change is higher now than it was several years ago. More people seem to feel the energies shifting, and we are feeling the energies shifting more.

I hope you feel like you are on a journey and are curious about where that journey leads. We are indeed moving farther down the path of that journey to remembering who we are. But first, I'd like to review where we have been.

In the beginning of this book I shared with you that the Twelve Rays are divided into three distinct groups. The first group of Rays is referred to as the Rays of Aspect. This group consists of the energy from the Source—or All That Is—that is our Divine Heritage. The second group, the Rays of Attributes, represents our human characteristics that enable us to have the unique experiences here in this dimension. The third group, the Rays of Soul Integration, consists of tools to help us to move forward in our evolution of Spirit here in this dimension.

I hope you have a better understanding of what the Rays are and how they benefit not only you personally but also all of humankind. Keep in mind that our focus here is on you, the individual. These Rays are intended to help you remember who you really are and to help guide you in this experience you are having.

There are many steps involved in lifting up the lower level energies of pain and suffering that we have known in our past. Each one of the Rays helps with a specific part of the process. I would summarize the entire process as transmuting the past, releasing feelings and emotions that are tied to experiences that no longer serve you. We are embracing the higher level of consciousness that we are and anchoring it into this dimension.

The purpose behind all of this is to move forward, to help evolve all that is manifest in this dimension. I know this sounds rather vague, and that is on purpose. You should be able to fill in the clarity yourself at this point. If this isn't real clear to you now, don't worry; everyone develops their understanding of this new reality according to their own timetable.

I have talked about how all the Rays come from a single, undifferentiated Source. The first three Rays, the Rays of Aspect, have a striking resemblance to the Trinity of Christian religions. The Rays of Attributes, Rays Four through Seven, provide support to particular personality types and soul purposes or life plans. The Seventh Ray, the Violet Flame, also serves as an energy to transmute lower-level energy. And then we come to the higher Rays, the Rays of Soul Integration, Rays Eight through Twelve. These are the new Rays that have only recently been available to humankind. They are not new in the sense that they have been recently created. Rather, they are new because they have only recently been made available for our use.

The Ninth and the Tenth Ray are used to connect with the soul-level consciousness and to anchor in the Body of Light. While discussing the Tenth Ray, I also introduced the Spiritual Microtron, the smallest portion of intelligent energy and the building block of everything that is manifest. The Eleventh and Twelfth Rays are discussed in the following chapters.

Opening to the New Awareness

All that you have read about and worked through up until this point has really been preparation for what we are now about to discuss and experience. You need to have achieved a certain level of progress with all the concepts and meditations that have so far been presented. The Team made this very clear to us, and I will share with you their comments about proceeding with the Eleventh and Twelfth Rays.

> The higher Rays that you are focused on are your tools to assist the Earth and that life experience of your own—no difference except for the focus and direction of the energy. We understand your desire to know more, to understand why we haven't discussed the Eleventh and Twelfth Rays. When your—your vibration has been cleared of the fear, when your beliefs have been opened, that time, that moment will come. But before— before experiencing those Rays, you must clear yourself, clear the baggage that you have accumulated from the illusions you have latched onto.
>
> When you can look at that mature self that has walked through the threshold of time and you can feel the innocence of that untarnished heart, then you will know that you are ready, and we already know. When you

can hold the Earth and feel yourself in its magnificence, when you can understand the energy that you possess, the power and strength that is yours and the love that you are capable of expressing, then you will be ready. You will be ready to not just read, not just talk; you will be ready to be that which you know you are.

Are you ready to be that which you know you are? If you encounter resistance within yourself as you proceed with the remaining material, come back to this section and ask yourself this question. If you are not yet ready to be that which you know you are, then simply go back and review the preceding chapters. This is not a race. There is no reward for finishing in the fastest time. There is, however, a wonderful reward for finishing. That reward is your understanding of the New Awareness.

How will you know when you have cleared away enough of the old fear, the old beliefs, the old baggage? Feel your heart. Let your heart guide you. Be honest with yourself. Are you ready to continue this journey, or do you still need some time to process, to release? Let your heart give you the answer. If you are honest with yourself, you will know when it is time to proceed.

CHAPTER 19

The Eleventh Ray

In an earlier chapter, I talked a little about change that is external to you, the individual. How are the people around you responding to the changes they see in you, changes that you yourself might not even notice? Now it is time to consider how you are responding to the changes within yourself.

The Eleventh Ray is about letting go of all the limiting beliefs about who and what you are. It is about letting go of the patterns you have formed over your lifetime that no longer serve you. It prepares you for what is coming next. I will have more to share about what is coming next when we discuss the Twelfth Ray. In this chapter, we will focus on the internal transition to the New Awareness.

Are you ready to continue your journey? Are you ready to shift out of your comfort zone and head into what may seem to be unchartered waters? I am not suggesting that you are about to uncover some wonderful new truth about who you are. I am asking you to remember how magnificent you truly are. The rewards of remembering your true self will be well worth the temporary discomfort you may feel releasing the parts of your past that, although they may seem comforting, may also be holding you back, keeping you from remembering.

Here is some advice from the Team.

> As you evolve and change, you find yourselves in a time of turmoil, a time of decision. And it is a dangerous time for the human entity, for it is a time to examine what are you, what do you want to be, which parts of yourself do not work for you. What is your goal, knowing goals change in this moment? What is your goal? What parts of you, your personality, your limits, must you let go of to move forward, to achieve, to get it done— what you know in your heart is your desire to achieve?
>
> So this time is a time of choice, of letting go, for each of you. What do

you choose to let go of, and what do you replace it with? We are here to offer you guidance and insight, yet you have choice. You can choose to integrate the knowledge you have been given or choose to walk away.

I hope you make the choice to integrate. From the Team's perspective, you can make either choice, and each is equally valid. However, from my perspective, which of course is way different from theirs, I hope you continue to integrate what they have shared with us.

Assuming that your choice is to continue your journey, the Team has some advice about possible pitfalls along the way.

You have been asked to integrate; to allow and surrender; to be wise to the new awareness of these energies, of your opportunities; to live drawing in this energy, this Spiritual Microtron, this Body of Light into your physical body and ever-so-slowly changing each molecule, each cell. And you will notice as you work with these higher Rays, these higher energies, you will move through periods of discomfort. You will notice change within your physical body. Pay attention to where you feel these changes, how your body reacts, for they will be signs of where you still have issues, where discomfort needs to be released—is asking to be released.

You will be opening to greater awareness. Your doors and opportunities will open around you. Pay attention, for some of these doors are not to be ventured into. Use your discernment. Use your intuitions. Pay attention and move in directions that raise your vibration and release those opportunities. Move away from those doors that try to lure you away from the light, for in this time of change, in this environment of polarity as you draw the light, so you also draw the shadows. Understand how ego will struggle to survive. Only feel, only allow, only surrender to what points you in the direction of love and joy.

Your physical body is indeed changing. It is adapting to your higher energetic levels, and there will be resistance. This resistance might present itself as discomfort within the body, and this is a very good indication that there is still work to be done. You are an energetic being, and as you raise your energy, you affect your physiology. We store emotions within the body, and the lower-level emotions like fear and anger and guilt are not compatible with your higher energetic level. Use the Eleventh Ray to transmute those pockets of resistance within your physical body. A little later in this section, I'll guide you through a meditation that will focus on just that.

The concept of discernment is very important. As you stand more in your individual power, you must rely more on your own personal discernment. It is up to you individually to figure out which directions to move in, which choices move you further toward your goals. There are choices you can make that will detour you or perhaps even send you in totally reverse directions. Use the Eleventh Ray to look for past patterns of behavior that are no longer serving you. Look at them and determine if they are entrenched patterns that need to be replaced with new ones. Perhaps they are merely old habits that can be simply released with intention.

Cultivate your discernment. Learn from your past choices and move in the direction that most supports your goals.

Expanding Limits

When we come into this world, we all experience the feeling of being only a part of our normal consciousness. Which normal consciousness am I referring to? I'm referring to the state of consciousness that you have before you jump into this reality, that state of consciousness that has a much different perspective than the limited one that most of us now have. Remember that no matter how much progress you have made in releasing your limitations in this dimension, you are still restricted in consciousness by the heaviness of the energy here.

You can see how being less than we normally are can lead initially to a bit of confusion. I'm sure many of us have heard about the notion that small children still seem to be connected to the higher dimensions. This is sometimes demonstrated by young children playing with their invisible friends. Well, their invisible friends are real. Sometimes young children have very accurate memories of their prior lives. As new arrivals to the planet, these lingering connections help us to make sense out of the mental confusion.

Over time, however, the children lose the ability to continue to see their special friends, and the memories of that past life begin to fade away, and rightly so. They need to begin to focus on their new experience here in this dimension.

We are only able to experience a small portion of our true identities because of the denseness of the energy here within this dimension. Within this lower level of energy, however, there is still room for expansion. There is still room to raise the energetic levels of ourselves and our environment. There is room to bring in more of ourselves, and that is what we are experiencing now. And the Twelve Rays are intended to help us accomplish that task.

Here is the Team's description of the opportunity that is now available to all of us to bring in more of who we are.

> *Our message is very simple. We have expressed it many times. Coming into this relative world in this physical body, you were a cup of energy with boundaries that you set as you entered this world. It is time to overflow the glass and expand your boundaries and understand what fills that cup and how it can exist beyond the boundaries that were set when you moved into this environment.*

You mean you can change the rules as you go along?

You can change whatever you decide to change. You have the power to remake yourself each and every moment. Just discover how that energy exists. You can exist beyond the limits of the cup. You're dynamic and changing if you let yourself be.

The Eleventh Ray is the energy to use to help us move through this transition. Interestingly, the Team has given us very little direct information about the Eleventh Ray. Here is what they had to say about it.

The Eleventh Ray is a bridge, a bridge to new awareness, to new horizons. It is the next level for humanity and Earth. You may picture it as an orange-pink, luminescent energy. A combination of the First, the Second, and the Fifth Rays, with of course the white light of Source added. It is very special, for it is the next era of living for humanity and for Earth. The First Ray is very penetrating, the Second Ray softens, and the Third is again more penetrating. Excuse me—let me correct myself. The Fifth Ray makes it more penetrating.

So, you may ask, what is it penetrating? What does it need to penetrate at this level? It is a remnant remover you could say. As the opportunity comes closer and as you approach that final cleansing, the final removal of the remnants of what has been will be cleared out.

That sounds pretty exciting—a new era of living for humanity and the Earth. Now you have an idea of where all of this work with the Twelve Rays is leading. Something big is happening, and like most major shifts, it is embraced a little bit at a time.

The concepts that Earth is round and revolves around the Sun took hundreds of years to be accepted and understood by the masses. Concepts like "you are a multidimensional being having a physical experience" are now finally beginning to be accepted on a much larger scale in a much shorter time frame. These types of shifts involve major changes to the human psyche.

The old beliefs need to be updated. The patterns of pain and suffering need to be released. These are some of the remnants that I believe the Team is talking about here. Let me remind you that when the Team uses the term cleansing, they really mean a transmuting of the energy into a higher frequency. Let's take a minute or two and feel the energy of this Eleventh Ray.

Stop, Feel, and Listen ♪♪

Allow yourself to relax. Take a gentle, deep breath and feel your calm breathing continue as you envision the orange-pink, luminescent energy of the Eleventh Ray. See it as it surrounds you, and with your intention, allow it to move through you. And for now, just briefly contemplate those old beliefs, those old patterns of fear and judgment, and see how easy it will be to move forward using this energy into the new era that has been announced. Allow that excitement to begin to build. And when you can feel the potential, when you can feel the energy rising up within you, gently open your eyes and return to this place and this time.

Allow me to once again suggest you write down any insights that may have occurred to you while you were processing this information.

How did that feel? Are you beginning to get really excited? I hope you can feel it. This is a lot to comprehend. If you feel that this is a little too overwhelming, just take your time with it. You can go back to any of the prior exercises and continue to work with them until you feel you are ready to move on.

Discussion

There are two interesting concepts in this information for me. The first is the introduction of the phrase "New Awareness." It is defined as the next level, the next era of living for humanity and the Earth. Does that mean we are on the brink of a really wonderful change of course for humankind and Earth? I think it means we have that possible choice available to us now. We are at a crossroads, and we can continue as is or choose differently.

You see how polarized the public is in the United States. Half of the people are for it, and half are against it. It really doesn't seem to make any difference what the "it" is. There is polarization everywhere. Is there a solution to the polarization? Yes, of course there is. What is it? Be darned if I know what it is. I just know there is one, and I am quite sure the New Awareness is part of the solution.

The other concept that I find most interesting is that we can use the Eleventh Ray as a remnant remover. Now, just what does that mean to you?

You might answer, "Well, I guess a remnant could be the last piece of something like a rug remnant." Perhaps you might envision it as an old stone chimney you see out in a field, and you know it used to be part of a structure that once stood there. You could define it as the last remaining piece of something that is just about all gone.

That is the way I think of it in this context. All of those are, of course, very descriptive of what a remnant is, but in this case I like to think of it as the last remaining piece. So what are these remnants the last remaining pieces of? They are the last pieces of what we have worked so hard to release, to transmute.

They may be the original foundations that allowed large structures to spring up from them. The structures are gone now. You have worked to release them using the other Rays. It is time now to remove the very last remaining pieces, the foundational pieces.

How do we do that? The Team has previously suggested that we may feel areas of discomfort in our physical bodies as we work to release the lower-level energies. I have included a guided journey to help you to connect with your body, and we will use the Eleventh Ray to help find the remnants that are still present in your physiology. Remember that there is consciousness at every level of your physical body. We are going to connect with that consciousness and allow it to show us where the remaining remnants are.

Now you may sense these remnants in a number of different ways. Allow yourself to be open to the information your body is about to communicate to you. When you sense the location of a remnant, I'm going to show you in the guided journey how you can transmute it. If it is not ready to transmute today, then you can make a mental note of it and move on. You can work with it later on your own.

This meditation is intended to help you connect with your physical body and to use that connection to understand where there are residual pockets of energy and emotion that need to be transmuted. If they are ready to be transmuted today, then we will let them shift. If they need further processing, then you will be able to work on that later on your own.

 ## The Eleventh Ray Meditation: REMOVING REMNANTS

Let's begin by putting down everything that you are holding or that may be in your lap and get into a nice comfortable position. Allow your feet to lie flat on the floor, or you may choose to fold them underneath you—whatever feels most comfortable to you. Allow your hands to lie comfortably in your lap or at your sides—again whatever is most comfortable for you. Take a gentle, deep breath, breathing in relaxation and exhaling any tension you may be feeling. Continue to breathe nicely and easily.

Now I would like you to see yourself in your sacred place. Pick the place that is most appropriate today for connecting with the consciousness of your physical body. You may choose the place where you meet with your guides and your teachers. Or you may select a place that you go to in your meditations, or perhaps you have a beautiful place to go when you just want to relax. Take a moment and choose the most appropriate place for you to go today to work with the Eleventh Ray.

Now bring your awareness to your feet and silently give your feet permission to relax. Silently say to yourself, "Relax my feet." Now move your awareness up to your legs and tell your legs to relax. Continuing to move along, tell your thighs to relax. Now tell your hips to relax. Continuing to move upward, giving your lower back permission to relax. Now relax your abdomen. Move your awareness into your chest and allow your chest to relax. Now the shoulders—tell your shoulders to relax. Now move to the face and tell all the muscles in your face to relax. And now your head—tell your head to relax.

Now scan your body from your feet to your head, and anywhere that you feel tension, stop and tell that part again to relax.

Now I would like you to visualize the Eleventh Ray, the luminescent pink and orange energy of the Eleventh Ray. Allow it to surround you and feel it almost like a blanket of energy all around you. Allow it to penetrate deep within your body, this beautiful pink and orange energy.

Now use your imagination to talk to the consciousness of your body. Ask your body to talk with you today and wait for a reply. You can say something like, "I am here today to help you raise up any and all remnants of lower-level emotions or thoughts. Are you willing to talk with me today?" Hopefully, you will receive a positive response. If you receive no response, simply ask again. If there is still no response, then just continue along. Once the body sees your intention, it may change its mind and want to actively participate.

If the body is communicating with you, ask it to show the areas that are holding on to remnants. Just state this as a request—something like, "Please show me where I am holding on to emotional remnants." Now scan your body again, beginning at your feet and notice where you feel a shift. This may be a heaviness or a change in color or temperature or even just a feeling that this part here needs to be worked with.

When you find a place to work with, you can physically move your hands to cover it, or you can simply imagine your hands cupping it, one hand above the area and one hand below the area. Now bring your awareness to that area and just focus on raising up that energy. You may see a color or a shape in your mind, and if you do, just continue to watch it and see what it does. When you can no longer see it, move on to the next area.

If there is no change to the area, then remember where it is, and you will come back to it later. Keep scanning and processing until all the areas have been worked with. I'll give you a couple of minutes now to complete the process.

(Wait three minutes.)

In a moment, we are going to begin our journey back to full, waking consciousness. Take the remaining time to finish up the area you are currently working with. If there are more areas to work with, you will have to save them for another time.

(Wait one minute.)

Now we will begin our journey back. I would like you to once again do a complete scan of your body from your feet to your head. Notice if there is any difference, and if there is a difference, notice what has changed.

When you have finished your scan, just notice how your body feels now. Remember the areas that were not ready to be released today. You will be able to work with them later when you repeat this process.

Now we will begin our journey back. I would like you to take a gentle, deep breath. And now as you focus on your gentle breathing, I would like you to gently wiggle your fingers and your toes. And as you are gently moving your fingers and your toes, I would like you to begin to allow your consciousness to become aware once again of the surrounding room. Become more and more aware of the place where you are. I would like you to take another gentle breath and, when you are ready, open your eyes and return to this place and this time. Welcome back.

Eleventh Ray Meditation: REMOVING REMNANTS
INSIGHTS

Insights: list as many as you can remember.

Main concepts: what is the subject matter behind the concepts?

Meaning for you: how do you interpret these insights?

How can you use this in your daily life?

Why is that helpful?

Sometimes the body will take this opportunity to share with you its feeling about your relationship. It may have felt neglected in the past. Or it may have been trying to communicate with you and may feel that you ignored it or didn't value its input. This may be the first time you have really been able to communicate so directly and clearly with it. Please take the time to hear what the body has to say and make every effort to sincerely acknowledge how much it supports you. Where would you be without it?

Sometimes when I lead this journey in live events, people experience resistance. If you experienced resistance when asking your body to cooperate with you, it needs to be addressed. The best way to address the resistance is to repeat the meditation, and at the point when you sense resistance, ask your body consciousness to share with you the reason for the resistance. There may be something that needs attention that you were unaware of. Take the time to figure out the source of the resistance and then work to eliminate it.

Some resistance is to be expected. This work with the Eleventh Ray might be deeper than you have done in the past. Resistance is the normal way we protect ourselves from change that is not well thought out. So when you encounter this resistance you are really being challenged to think about what you are changing. Is this really what you want, and is this really what you are ready for? It is reasonable then, if you are not 100 percent sure about the change, to proceed cautiously with it. If you are not yet ready to transmute it all the way, you can always come back to it when you have considered the impact of the change further.

This work with the Eleventh Ray, this transmuting of the remaining remnants, is an ongoing process. I can't tell you how long it will or should take. I am not sure we should even have the expectation that we will ever complete it in this current incarnation.

I recommend that you repeat this meditation several times. The first reason to do this is of course to process any remnants that you didn't get to transmute the first time. Just spend more time with a reluctant remnant. Dialogue more with it until you can convince it that its service to you is complete and that you understand the full impact of transmuting it. Make sure to thank it for its service as you transmute it. The second reason to repeat this meditation is that it is much like peeling the layers of an onion. You have to release the outer portions to get all the way down to the center. It takes repetition and focused attention to get closer and closer to that last piece.

You don't have to wait until all the remnants have been removed before you move on to the Twelfth Ray. These two Rays work hand in hand with each other. In the next section, you will get an introduction to the Twelfth Ray, but the actual experience of the Twelfth Ray will be an ongoing process of opening to it.

There is no one way to proceed from this point. Based on your individual experiences so far, you may choose to work more with the Eleventh Ray before moving on. You may wish to proceed to the next chapter and acquaint yourself with the material but not engage the Twelfth Ray directly. Or you may feel totally comfortable in moving forward and working with both Rays together. Feel free to find what works best for you. And when you are ready, I invite you to turn to the next chapter.

Summary and Key Concepts

- We are all living in a time of great change. I know you have probably heard that before. The Twelve Rays offer additional opportunities for personal change.
- Resistance is the normal way we protect ourselves from change that is not well thought out.
- The Eleventh Ray is referred to as the Bridge to the New Awareness, and the Twelfth Ray is the New Awareness.
- Use the Eleventh Ray as a remnant remover. What type of remnant am I referring to? Resistance to moving forward is a good example.
- The New Awareness is ours to experience.

Learnings

- We come into this experience with defined limits. These limits are arbitrary and tailored to our intentions within this life experience. Working with the Twelve Rays provides an opportunity to move beyond those original limitations. There is nothing that prevents you from embracing expanded beliefs about yourself and this reality.
- Opening to the New Awareness requires a certain personal energetic level which requires a certain level of personal effort. Working with the Twelve Rays is one way to raise your energetic level.

CHAPTER 20

The Twelfth Ray

I would like to begin this section with a short, recent passage from the Team.

> *You live in a time, a pace of evolution unlike any before, ready and anxious to receive a message, new, fresh, a message of hope and healing available to each and every human on Earth, available to all no matter their status, no matter their despair.*

The New Awareness is a message of hope and healing and much, much more. It is a message of new potential, of new experiences that have never before been available in this dimension. I know that is a very broad and sweeping statement. Understand that any description of the New Awareness is an understatement because I really can't even begin to comprehend what we are capable of in this dimension. What I do know is that we have the opportunity to choose hope over despair, to choose empowerment over fear, to choose love over everything else.

That is how I would like to set the stage for our discussion of the New Awareness. Imagine what you can't imagine. How do you do that? Release all the limitations of how you see life on Earth and then imagine that there is more. How do you conceive of what the more is? Use your imagination, and then when your imagination reaches its limits, imagine what is beyond those limits. I am not suggesting that this is easy. But I hope you are getting as excited about it as I am.

When the Team first introduced us to the Twelfth Ray, they gave us very little information. The New Awareness isn't something that can be succinctly described. It is much bigger than that. But the Team did give us a good starting point. Here is what they had to say directly about the Twelfth Ray.

And now the Twelfth Ray. The Eleventh Ray was a Bridge to New Awareness, the Twelfth Ray is New Awareness. It is a combination of all Rays, all possibilities. See it as a golden, luminescent energy, and it is the best of the Rays to bring in when you are seeking New Awareness. It is literally an embodiment of all the Rays.

A most powerful way to use it is to create a vortex or column of energy around yourself or around your planet; immerse yourself into this energy and send it into the Earth. The vibration from this Ray as you direct it, whether to yourself or to Earth, is most harmonizing and will increase the vibration of wherever it is directed.

We have talked many times about the tapestry that each of you creates, a weave of energy, some weaves more intricate, some more allowing. And as you work with these Rays, the higher Rays along with the other Rays, you create a melody. You change the weave. You raise the vibrations of each and every soul.

If you are like me, I felt like I wanted to know more after receiving the above description. The more comes when you are ready to embrace it. For us, it took a while. My hope is that your focused effort to work with the energy of the Rays and the Twelfth Ray in particular, this "embodiment of all the Rays," will enable you to move at your own speed.

The analogy of the tapestry is one that the Team loves to use. This tapestry is energetic in nature and is the summation of our experiences in this dimension. Sometimes there are gaps or tears in it, and we can work to mend these areas. In other places, there is low-level energy that can be replaced with higher-level energy, and that is what the Team is mentioning here, the raising of the energetic levels of whatever part of the tapestry we are working with.

Let's take a couple of minutes and get acquainted with the energies of the Twelfth Ray.

Stop, Feel, and Listen

Place yourself in a comfortable position with your feet flat on the floor or tucked underneath you. Take a gentle breath feeling the relaxing energy of this deep breath entering into your lungs and breathe out any tension or stress you may be feeling. Continue your gentle, rhythmic breathing. Envision a vortex or column of golden, luminescent energy above you and direct it to descend and surround you. Feel its harmonizing effects as you direct it through you into the Earth. Feel your energetic vibration rise as you embrace its energy.

Imagine your beautiful tapestry that you have created through all of your earthly experiences. See how rich and full it is and allow the energy of this Ray to raise the vibration of your entire tapestry. See it become more vibrant and colorful right before you.

Work with it as long as you choose. When you are ready to return to this dimension, take a gentle, deep breath and allow your consciousness to begin to return to your physical body. Gently move your fingers and your toes, allowing your consciousness to fully return to your physical body. And when you are ready, gently open your eyes and return to this place and this time. Welcome back.

For this last time, write down any insights that may have occurred to you while you were processing this information.

The experience of this Ray will deepen each time you work with it. I encourage you to repeat this quick meditation often. The effort you expend here will be well worth it and will help you in your progress to opening to the New Awareness.

Connection

The New Awareness starts with connection. When we come into this world, it is easy to feel disconnected. It is easy to feel like we have been dropped off and we are on our own, but this is an illusion. It is, however, an illusion with purpose. Here in this dimension of dense energy, we are infused with the elements of physical life. Things appear to be solid. Yet the scientists are now telling us that atoms are mostly made up of space. We are governed by the rules of time, but is there really such a thing as time, or is it also just an illusion? If we could instantaneously manifest anything, how would that be different than our current experience of personal achievement?

The purpose of this illusion then is to experience ourselves as we never have. We see our creations taking shape over time, and we can enjoy the process of making things through our own individual labor. This is why the illusion of separation makes sense. It allows us to enjoy the process of individual creation over time.

The illusion of separation is very strong, and it comes with certain attributes that affect us all, and some of these attributes can be experienced as unpleasant. One of those unpleasant attributes is loneliness. In our higher levels of consciousness, it is impossible to feel lonely. We are constantly connected. Again, we come here to this dimension for the experience. How better to appreciate the connection to each other than to experience the separation?

There comes a time, however, when it is possible to move beyond the illusion of separation, and this is the beginning of our understanding of the New Awareness.

The higher Rays allow us to remember that connection. When we are ready to embrace the understanding of the connection, then we are ready to move into the New Awareness.

Interestingly enough, that aha moment, that understanding of our connectedness came for me just a little over a year ago, and it came in the middle of a session with the Team.

> *The challenge for most is the forgetfulness of the connection that they have, the masters of creativity that they are, their right to choose their expression rather than be a victim of it.*

Our physical—this is a question—our physical existence, the expression of who we are in this dimension, it is constantly supported by our connection with our higher self. Is that correct?

> *As long as you have life, you have a connection.*

And when the connection is withdrawn, that is when the life is withdrawn. Is that correct?

> *That would be correct.*

Do you know I never got that until just now? Can you believe that?

> *See how you have grown? In this lifetime, for all of the questioning, for all of the impatience that you have had, for your questioning of why it has taken so long in this lifetime for you to get where you are—celebrate the victory, for you have worked many lifetimes to understand what you say you now have an understanding of. We celebrate every victory in your expression. We celebrate through the connection, through your communication of Spirit, through every pain and every sense of harmony and peace. You are Spirit. Your physicalness is merely an expression.*
>
> *This is your worldly revolution to understand that you need not [experience] pain in order to evolve, you need not hurt, and you need not forget who you are. Your world can empower itself to express and remember.*
>
> *Your world acknowledges Spirit, but oftentimes fails to acknowledge the continual connection.*

I remember this session very well, and I must admit I felt a little thickheaded when I came to this realization. I wondered why it had taken me so long to get to this realization. Oh well. The important thing is that I came to it. From this exchange, I came to the realization that we are each constant expressions of our higher selves. There is really no need to create that connection because there has never been an interruption. If there had been a disconnection, we would no longer be here.

There is, however, a denial of that connection. I hope you can see that there was a time and a place for that denial, but now the opportunity exists to release that denial and embrace our connection. As we attempt to embrace our connections with our higher selves, we have to deal with the fear that is the basis of that denial. Here is how the Team describes that fear.

There is a fear of acknowledging Spirit as self, as the primary life force. And there are those in your world that are actively working to disempower that connection. We simply tell you that as you remember your connection, understand the significance of acknowledging that connection and choose to acknowledge it through a harmonious expression, that you empower that expression. You sensitize yourself as a creator. You draw into your expression through that acknowledgment of that greater perspective a broader—a broader choice, a strength, a greater joy.

Remember that you are the expression the Team is talking about. You are the one being empowered as you acknowledge your connection to Spirit.

I hope that your work with the Twelve Rays has helped you to release much if not all of the fear of embracing your connection with your higher self. You have come this far to move into the New Awareness, not to fall back into denial. If you feel that there is still fear present within you, go back and work some more with the Ninth and the Tenth Rays. Work with them to embrace your connection to your soul-level consciousness and your Body of Light. Use the Tenth Ray to anchor the higher energies of the Body of Light into your physical body and allow yourself to open to these new perspectives.

As you continue to move forward into the New Awareness, there are adjustments to your thinking, to your perceptions of reality that you will need to make. We often talk about the concept of releasing lower-level emotions that hold us down. When you get to this stage of awareness, it is time to start understanding energy concepts differently. These lower-level energies need to be transformed. We don't really release them, but there is a feeling of release as they shift to a higher level.

Are you ready to think differently? Are you ready for some new concepts?

You must throw away the old terms and come up with new and better ways. If you are ready to talk about new concepts, then you are ready to replace terminology with new thought.

You are whole, have been whole, will maintain a wholeness throughout your existence; therefore, pain and discord—disease—cannot be released, cannot be discarded, must be evolved, must be transformed, must be elevated.

The concept of release and the concept of attachment are old terms. It's time now to understand, to own who you are, the wholeness of your being. You manifest in your being, in your emotional and physical makeup, that which you believe, that which you choose, that which you acquire through experience. But you can evolve that thought—that manifested thought—to create, elevate, morph, and change whatever you can believe to be true.

So we present to you today the concept of Manifested Evolution through change in thought. For as you change thought, your energy changes. And as you are energy, as that is your reality, physical change takes place not to be released but to be evolved. And as you elevate that energy, those vibrations, your thought becomes lighter, less dense, which appears to be felt as a release when in fact if you were to release you would be less than whole. And since you are whole, it is not possible to release. Why would you want to release and be less than you are?

It is by choice that you have, as a human race, focused on discord, disease, [and] negativity, and your resurrection [is] dependent on a pattern change, a thought change, an empowerment. To own who you are, own the power that you have to create, evolve; to reflect on your experiences in new ways; to take the hurt, the pain, the judgment, and discord and raise it up, elevate it within your own being; to make a decision to see, to live, to live with those experiences in new ways.

To deny your past—any of your past—is to separate yourself from truth. And to live and continue to live with pain, disease, discord, judgment, guilt, shame with all the burdens that you and your human race embrace so dearly is to deny—deny the sight, deny the perspective of light, of love, of wholeness.

So a new concept moving away from the thought that somehow these ailments, these oppressions, these chains, the chains that you so dearly embrace, have been inflicted upon you from outside yourself—that thought must evolve. You are the creator of your own experience. You must own your experience.

There are a few concepts here that need to be discussed a little more deeply. The first one is the concept of being whole. I believe this to be a fundamental new concept. The Team is insisting that we are whole and have always been whole. That means we are not broken. It means we are not evolving our souls. It means we are not finding our way back to the Source. We simply are whole, and we have always been whole. All of the imperfections that we see around us are our own choices, and we have the power to evolve them, all of them. We do not release lower-level energies that are created through our experiences of pain and suffering and disease; we transmute them to a higher level within our experience.

The concept of Manifested Evolution is not about the evolution of our souls, but the evolution of our experiences here on Earth. We can change our beliefs and thereby change our experiences here. I believe the Team is suggesting that the time is now to change our thinking. They say our "resurrection is dependent on a pattern change, a thought change, an empowerment." I agree with them that pain and disease and judgment and all the rest of the suffering that we see all around us have been our focus.

It is time to change the old pattern. Our resurrection depends on it. The new pattern recognizes our connection to Spirit. It recognizes that this experience can be an experience of love and joy and happiness. It recognizes that we are the creators of our own experiences. It is a pattern of personal empowerment.

Personal Empowerment

We must become the creators of the New Awareness in order to experience it. We do that by changing our thought patterns, and we change our thought patterns through personal empowerment. The Team has some guidance regarding personal empowerment.

> And there is one more, one more piece of knowledge. On your journey into exploring and remembering what already exists, the knowledge with you, we have touched on another concept here, the soul merge, which in ancient wisdom is known as the third initiation. And we tell you this, the opportunities have opened up for your planet. What was true, the structures that were defined from many years ago have opened and are available.
>
> There is no ceremony, no formal initiation, except for your own awareness and opening process. Know now that you each hold the key to transform at your own choosing. We can certainly discuss ancient wisdom; it had its place. It served its purpose, but know now the power you possess at the creative level is available on Earth today as never before.
>
> You have selected us as your team in a very careful[ly] thought [out], purposeful manner. There is no accident, and each of us steps you up through the various levels of awareness. And with each step, you initiate yourself. You draw closer to bringing a divine wholeness of spirit into your physical structure and, by doing so, manifest for Earth a higher level of living and existence.

This is quite a declaration. The energies have shifted so much that the old structures of initiation have shifted. The old hierarchy has been replaced by self-initiation. How is that for personal empowerment? The process of initiation is now in your hands.

What do we do with this newly found personal empowerment? The simple answer is anything that we choose. Can you really continue on the way you have been going? Or is there a new you that you would like to put together, to assemble. As you might imagine, the Team has some comments about the new you.

You actually allow a reconstruction of self in your world. You can begin to draw off of that greater base of power of your higher self. You came into your world to experience certain aspects of yourself. But as you grow and evolve and when you get to that point that you can remember who you are and that connection to Spirit, you have the capacity to change elements of yourself that you desire to make changes to. That's a radical statement of personal empowerment.

Many would like you to believe you come into this world and what you have you have and you are stuck with. I tell you now that you change; you have the capacity to change as you understand your right to make those changes, and there is no restriction, no law in the greater dimensions that will deny you. You have physical laws that you must work through, emotional restrictions that you place upon yourself, but understand you have the power to be whatever you choose to be in your expression.

It's not so complicated. We have always tried to communicate to you in very simple, easy, straightforward ways. We do that with purpose. Empowerment is simply a matter of choice.

Are you ready to embrace the concept that "you have the power to be whatever you choose to be in your expression"? Once you reach a certain level of awareness, you have the power to change those aspects of yourself that you no longer need, and you can add aspects of yourself that were not present before. How is that for personal empowerment? It is there for you when you choose to accept it. As the Team states, it "is simply a matter of choice." This personal empowerment is another fundamental aspect of the New Awareness.

We now have the opportunity to create harmony in this environment without the use of conflict. At this level of awareness, we can begin to create harmony through empowerment and choice. Once again, the Team explains how this works.

Well, you are suggesting now to find harmony through evolution rather than conflict.

Right. And that evolution is empowerment and choice.

Would that be the New Awareness?

It is a New Awareness. It is stepping into that, that energy. It is not discarding any of the energy. You can imagine that Ray of light—a full band of Ray, of light—moving into you, moving into your physical, spiritual, and emotional bodies on Earth. You choose whatever you set your intention to choose. You draw to you what you feel you need. We are asking you to focus on the energies available in the Tenth, Eleventh, and Twelfth Rays, to bridge yourself to a new way of being, a new way of living, connected, connected.

When you can fully embrace the belief, the knowing, being connected,
then you can immediately evolve the energies in your experience.

We are drawn back to the concept of being constantly connected to our higher consciousness and the awareness and abilities that realization brings with it. It has taken us some time to work through all of these Rays and arrive at this level of awareness. What a reward for all the effort and hard work! We can now begin to immediately evolve the energies in our experience. I wish I could describe this in greater detail to you, but at this point, I can only suggest that you have to experience this in your own way. Remember that we are talking about the energies from our past experiences as well as our current and future experiences.

I hope you can envision the magnitude of this New Awareness. We are just beginning to comprehend the possibilities that lie before us. What an exciting time to be here on Earth and witness the unfolding of the New Awareness.

 Discussion

As you worked with each of these chapters in this book, you had to make your own way to the point of being able to work with these higher Rays. This really is where the rubber meets the road. I realize that everyone has their own way of working with the Rays, and some are going to progress faster than others. My point is that you need to be properly prepared to work with the Twelfth Ray since it is the summation of all the Rays.

It has been a long journey to the Twelfth Ray, and as you can see, there is really not that much information about the Twelfth Ray that was originally given. There is, however, some more recent information that we have received, and I will try to synthesize that for you now.

The first concept to talk about is the connection to one's higher self. Using the Ninth Ray, we established our soul-level connections that in reality have never been severed. We just have the illusion that we need to reestablish them. And even if we always felt connected—and I can tell you that I haven't felt always connected; actually until recently, it has been quite the opposite—we can use the Ninth Ray to strengthen that connection. Then we use the Tenth Ray to anchor our Bodies of Light to our physical bodies. This starts to raise our individual energetic levels even higher. Working with the Eleventh Ray helps you to shift your long-held beliefs about yourself. It helps you to expand the limits that have felt so comfortable up until now.

The Twelfth Ray requires your conscious recognition of your connection to your higher self, for this is where you draw your new abilities from. You need to be released from the fear of your own personal power. When you are ready to empower yourself, you can begin to reconstruct yourself. You have the ability to reconfigure your personality. You can release the old characteristics that allowed you to connect with and experience those memories that you needed to evolve to a higher energetic level. And you can bring in new personal characteristics that will support you as you create your New Awareness.

It is time for all of us to embrace some new concepts. I have often described the process of releasing the lower-level energies of our experiences as just that, a release. What we are really doing, however, is shifting these energies, evolving them to a higher level. The Team has sometimes referred to this process as cleansing, and by that, they mean the removal of the lower-level emotions of pain, suffering, and other negative emotions that these energies are connected to. So we now recognize that we don't really ever release experiences, but rather we evolve them to a higher energetic level. I hope that makes sense to you.

This means that you never really release those painful and fearful experiences from your past. They remain a part of your experience. The difference is that they no longer carry the feelings of pain and suffering. Those emotions have been evolved through your higher-level understanding—the understanding that you don't need to carry those lower-level emotions around with you anymore.

The next new concept is it is time to move forward. A lot of information has been given in the past that is frankly out of date. The energies have shifted. There are energies that are available now that were not available in the past. The level of personal empowerment that is available to all of us now far surpasses what was available in the past. What does that mean to you? It means you have the ability to progress faster in one lifetime now than it would have taken you in several lifetimes in the past. And that is a good thing.

The next concept—and this is really important when it comes to personal empowerment—is that past lives, the entire notion of past lives, is outdated. Past lives are not past. They are alive and available to access anytime you choose. I'm not going to spend a lot of time on that topic here. Perhaps there needs to be a book on the new understanding of past lives, which I refer to as aspects of your soul's personality. Yes, your soul does have a personality.

There are more new concepts, but I am going to leave it at that for now.

We have the concept of connection, the new concepts, and now the notion of a paradigm shift. We are shifting out of the paradigm of spiritual progress through pain and suffering to a new one that states that spiritual progress can be achieved through grace and ease. The Team uses the words empowerment and choice. So we spiritually progress through personal empowerment and choice. We have talked a little bit about this paradigm shift before. It seems to me that these higher Rays set the stage for us to embrace this new paradigm.

If you are ready to experience the Twelfth Ray, then let's proceed.

The Twelfth Ray Meditation: NEW AWARENESS

Let's begin by getting comfortable. Arrange your arms and your legs, so you are relaxed and comfortable. Take a gentle, deep breath and, as you do, allow your eyes to close. Breathe in the relaxing fresh air and exhale out any tension or stress you may be feeling. Continue breathing nice, rhythmic breaths. Just allow yourself to relax deeper and deeper as you listen to my voice.

We are going to begin our journey today by going to your sacred place. I would like you to think about which place would be most appropriate for you to work with the Twelfth Ray. Choose a place that you have perhaps been to before, either in meditation or in real life. Or you may choose a place that you have only dreamt about. Choose a place where it will be easy for you to lose your limited beliefs about who and what you really are. Choose a place that will allow you to see things that are grand and beautiful.

Allow yourself to be there now. Feel how safe and relaxing and comfortable it feels to be here in your sacred place. Look around at all the beauty that surrounds you. You may see colorful flowers and trees. You may see beautiful mountains or hills in the distance. Perhaps there is a lake or a stream or maybe even an ocean nearby. Simply allow the scenery to take shape in front of you. Use your focused attention to create a unique landscape for all to behold. Now add to this beautiful landscape the perfume of the blossoms on the flowers and the trees. Add also the beautiful songs of the wind rustling through the leaves and water splashing on the shore, the birds calling in the wind. Allow this feeling of peace and beauty and calm to move into you. Feel the beauty of your own creation.

And now, envision the Twelfth Ray as a golden column of light descending upon you. Allow it to fully surround you and invite it to move fully through you. This golden light is the energy of the New Awareness. Remember your connection to those levels of consciousness that you have experienced before. Feel your connection to your physical body and the 50 trillion cells within it, each one with its own individual consciousness. Feel your connection with your inner guidance, your Body of Light, and your soul-level consciousness. Feel your connection with your higher self and with All That Is.

And as you feel this connection, imagine before you our solar system. See the Sun in the middle and the planets revolving around it. And as you look at the planets, find the ones that interest you and allow yourself to travel to them. Match their speed as they rotate around the Sun. I'll give you a minute to explore.

(Wait one minute.)

When you have visited the ones of interest to you, direct your awareness to our planet. Direct your awareness to Earth. Now move toward it. See yourself right next to it. Imagine it to be about the size of a soccer ball, maybe a little smaller.

Now I would like you to imagine holding Earth in your lap with your hands. That's right. See your hands around it there in your lap. Now direct the Twelfth Ray down your arms and out through your hands. Feel the energy between your hands. Good.

Now, direct the energy toward Mother Earth and surround the planet with the Twelfth Ray. See the golden light move all over the planet and send it deep into Mother Earth so that all living and nonliving things feel the energy of the Twelfth Ray, the energy of the New Awareness.

Now imagine life being different here on the planet. Imagine a new way of sharing and caring. Imagine a world in harmony, filled with love for all of its inhabitants. What does that look like to you? What does that feel like to you? Take a few minutes to allow that picture to unfold before you.

(Wait two minutes.)

Now in a minute, you will begin your journey back. Take this remaining time to feel the beauty of this peaceful, lush Earth. Move this image into your heart and allow this beauty and peace and joy to fill your heart. This is your New Awareness. You are the creator of your own New Awareness. Be fearless as you move through this vision of what is to come. Be fearless in envisioning a New Awareness for Mother Earth and all of her inhabitants. This is a future that we all can help to become real.

Now see yourself back in your sacred place. Allow the memory of all that you have seen and felt and experienced to come back with you. Feel yourself still surrounded by the energy of the Twelfth Ray, the energy of the New Awareness. Realize that you are the creator of the New Awareness, and with this experience, with this vision firmly implanted in your mind, you are free to begin to create it in your physical life. You are free to make it part of your physical experience.

Now take a gentle, deep breath. Begin to allow your consciousness to return to your physical body. As you continue to gently breathe, slowly move your fingers and your toes. And as you become aware of your fingers and your toes, connect once again with your arms and your legs. Allow your consciousness to now fully return to your physical body and, when you are ready, gently and slowly open your eyes and return to this place and this time. Welcome back.

Twelfth Ray Meditation: NEW AWARENESS
INSIGHTS

Insights: list as many as you can remember.

_____

_____

_____

_____

Main concepts: what is the subject matter behind the concepts?

_____

_____

_____

_____

Meaning for you: how do you interpret these insights?

_____

_____

_____

_____

How can you use this in your daily life?

_____

_____

_____

_____

Why is that helpful?

_____

_____

_____

_____

This meditation is generally considered easier than the Eleventh Ray meditation. People often experience less resistance. It seems that it is easier to envision something new and wonderful in the future than shift the parts of your consciousness that have limited you in the past.

The Eleventh Ray meditation required a different level of commitment at a deeper level. And it requires the desire to move beyond beliefs and experiences that we have held for such a long time. Many of these deeper beliefs have been our closest friends for lifetime upon lifetime. It is not easy to say goodbye to old friends.

When you remember the resistance that you experienced with the Eleventh Ray meditation, I hope you realize that there is still work to be done. Now, there is no established timetable to complete that work. I think it is reasonable to assume that this is not going to be completed in the next month or six months or perhaps even within the next year. Please don't hold an expectation that you should complete the work with these higher Rays in any particular time frame. Everyone needs to progress at their own speed. This is not a race. You don't get extra points for finishing the fastest. As a matter of fact, it would probably be better to not look at this as a goal at all. See it more as a journey and just enjoy the journey.

As I end this chapter, allow me to offer some advice to you. It has been a long journey through the Rays. You have progressed at your own speed, the speed that you have felt was best for you. Now is a good time to evaluate your experience with this information. Give yourself time to process all that you have been exposed to. You may want to go back and review certain parts of the Rays. I certainly recommend that you continue to work with the Eleventh and the Twelfth Rays. As you experience your New Awareness, I encourage you to step into your power and create your New Awareness with love, compassion, and joy.

Summary and Key Concepts

- Our physical reality allows us to experience certain conditions that do not exist in the other dimensions in which we have our consciousness. We often refer to these conditions as illusions because they can only be experienced here.
- Separation is one of those so-called illusions. We see ourselves in this dimension as stand-alone individuals.
- There is purpose in this illusion. We get to experience ourselves as creators over time. In the other dimensions, creation takes place instantaneously.
- Pain, suffering, and difficulty are also illusions.
- We come to this reality to experience what cannot be experienced elsewhere.
- The New Awareness is ours to discover. Part of it involves moving forward with the understanding of these illusions.

Learnings

- We are Spirit. Our physicality is merely an expression.
- We need not experience pain in order to evolve. We need not hurt, nor forget who we are. We can empower ourselves to remember and embrace our Divine Heritage as creators of our own realities.
- We are constantly being projected into this reality by our whole selves. We have always been connected to our whole selves. When the connection is withdrawn, that is a definition of death.
- The New Awareness is ours to create. What will it be like? Mostly likely it will be beyond our current human imaginations.

CHAPTER 21

My New Awareness

My path to my personal New Awareness was a long one, which started out in Buffalo, New York, over sixty years ago. I was married at a young age and completed my college education as a young husband and father. But even at that early age, I felt drawn by unknown forces. I felt the desire to live and work in Germany. And so I did. That is where I had my first profound experience with something beyond my awareness. As the train pulled out of the Cologne station heading for our new home just outside of Bremen, I looked around at the tiny vegetable gardens that were on the side of the tracks, a sight that I had never seen before, and one thought came into my mind—"home."

After two years of living and working in Germany as an English teacher, we returned home, and I completed my graduate studies. That led to a career in the rapidly exploding field of computer programming. I must confess that I found this work to be creative and comfortable at the same time. I felt I was good at it. So we bought a house and settled in with our three children.

But I felt there was more. I felt drawn to find that more. After twenty years of marriage, I divorced, moved out of Buffalo, and eventually settled in Charlotte, North Carolina, where I live today. I originally moved here to continue my career in computer banking and landed what I thought was the best job I ever had. That lasted three years, and it was indeed very interesting, but it was a continuation of my roller-coaster corporate ride. I decided I'd had enough of corporate life. I struck out on a new path and opened a wellness center that I named Phoenix Rising, the metaphor of the phoenix being too good to pass up. This turned out to be a beacon for Julie. Our paths first crossed at Phoenix Rising, and this is where we first met the Team.

I had been resisting meditation. I had been resisting the belief in reincarnation. It turned out that my resistance was based in fear. Being a recovering Catholic, the notion of eternal life with God in heaven sounded … well, frankly, a little boring. It sounded like just hanging around for eternity telling God how great He is. I now realize that I resisted meditation because I was afraid of opening up my Pandora's box. I had no idea what I would find there. All of this came to a head when we had the first session with the Team.

I remember that first session with the Team. I felt like the proverbial deer in the headlights. What the heck do we do now? They advised us to just be patient and process the information that they were providing. I turned to Julie after that first meeting with them and said, "Well, that was pretty mind-blowing." What were we supposed to do with this opportunity? We had established direct contact through Julie with entities who were communicating from a different dimension.

One of my first thoughts was that they were communicating with us so that together we could save the world. Might as well start out big. Then I soon came to realize that they were helping us to achieve our goals that we had established for this life experience. That might eventually produce some information that could be shared for the benefit of others. But we had to focus on our own journeys first, and that is what I have recommended to you throughout this entire book. Focus on your own work first.

I had to address my fears about opening up to what was inside of me. I had to accept that I alone am responsible for what I experience in my life. I had to accept the responsibility for creating my own reality. If you feel the fear of going inside and taking responsibility for your life, rest assured that it was a major issue for me. You have your own group of guides and teachers that, hopefully, you have connected with by now. You have your own plan for your lifetime. Focus on your own goals, and you will achieve them, and those around you will notice those achievements. Lead by your own actions.

My life has been quite a journey with its ups and downs. I can remember sometimes feeling on top of the world and other times feeling buried underneath the weight of this reality. I am proud of some of my accomplishments and ashamed of some of my deeds. I think I am not alone with these mixed emotions. I believe I am making more progress in this lifetime than I have in several other lifetimes. And when I say progress, what I am really referring to is cleaning up my personal reincarnational baggage. And in the process of transmuting all that emotional residue from previous lifetimes, I believe I am laying the foundation for the next step, the next chapter in my personal reincarnational journey.

The Team helped me to embrace all of the baggage from my past experiences by telling me quite bluntly about some of those past lives.

You have had many experiences, and each has served you. You have been a beggar. You have been a prince. You have held a saber in your hand and have ridden with men and killed and been killed. You witnessed so much persecution. You desired to experience from the perspective of others what you could not understand. And you moved far away into the passion of war, of judgment, of ego, of dominance. And try as you did to come back to love, you felt sorrow and grief. Let go of the fear. Accept all that you have been.

I could go into more specific examples, but I think you get the meaning. In order to transmute these experiences, it is necessary to connect to them, accept them, and then move beyond them. The Twelve Rays are the tools that we offer at this time to help anyone who is willing to move beyond their fear and accept all that they have been.

Your New Awareness

There are many metaphors that I use to help get across the idea that humankind is on the brink of a significant shift in what we are capable of experiencing here in this dimension. I sometimes say, "We are not in Kansas anymore, Toto," making reference to Dorothy's realization in the *Wizard of Oz* that something dramatic had shifted in their reality. Or I like the analogy from a famous World War I song—"How ya gonna keep 'em down on the farm after they've seen Paree"—again a reference to a shift in perspective. When you work with the Rays, when you transmute the reincarnational baggage that you have been carrying from lifetime to lifetime, when you connect with your whole self and bring in your Body of Light, all of this leads you to your New Awareness.

As you moved through this book and worked with each of the exercises that were presented, you gained awareness of a different perspective. It doesn't matter if you are a beginner at personal spiritual development. It doesn't matter that you still have some reservations about the concept of reincarnation. It doesn't matter that you didn't hear voices or see beautiful images of places beyond this dimension and the entities who exist there. Maybe you got some of it but not all of it. Some is better than nothing at all. Or maybe your life has been profoundly impacted by your experiences. Whatever your experience was, you are certainly in a different place now than when you first opened the book.

Throughout this book, we have discussed the foundational concept that you are more. The Team, Julie, and I presented tools to help you remember your connection with the part of you that we refer to as your whole self. We introduced the concept of the Body of Light. We provided exercises to help you anchor the Body of Light into your physical body. The Body of Light is one of the most exciting aspects of the Twelve Rays. Think of the potential that the Body of Light presents when anchored into your physical body. I strongly suggest that you take the time and go back and review the chapter on the Body of Light.

The ability to transmute the emotional baggage that we have created from lifetime to lifetime is essential to moving forward to higher energetic levels of existence. I cannot stress enough the benefits that you will reap by transmuting this lower-level energy. Let me use a small metaphor to help explain the source of what I have referred to as reincarnational baggage.

Reincarnational Baggage
(OR STUFF THAT WE SO LOVE TO CLING TO)

Think of a beautiful national park—Yellowstone maybe, although I've never been there. Now think of planning a visit to that park. You want to pack gear, hiking boots, raincoats, sweaters, backpacks, and so forth. Then there is activity-related equipment like fishing poles, life vests, a kayak, and so on. Then there are provisions, plenty to eat and drink. And each journey you take into the park, you enjoy what the park willingly offers you—the fresh air, the lakes and streams, the beautiful vistas, the opportunity to get away from it all.

Some folks leave the park untouched each time they leave. They take all of what they have consumed and recycle anything that could be considered trash. Others leave their markings behind. Perhaps they leave trash. Perhaps they catch fish and deplete the lakes and streams. Some chop wood and make fires and leave the ashes behind. Some pick the flowers and prevent new seeds from being spread. Sooner or later, everyone needs to go back and pick up their trash, recycle it, and restore what they have consumed. Otherwise, the park cannot sustain itself.

Sooner or later, we all need to go back and retrieve our trash that we have accumulated through our many visits to this dimension. We need to transmute whatever low-level emotional energy we have created through fear and anger and all other emotions not based in love. We don't have to do this in one single visit; the timing is totally left up to us.

Actually, we are not forced to go back and do it at all. It is a choice. There are, however, significant benefits in transmuting as much as possible before moving onto the next reincarnational level. And as we transmute what we have left behind, we lay a new foundation for what is yet to come.

Some experts in past-life regression believe you begin each incarnation with the beliefs that you died with. This makes some sense to me, but I think there is probably more to it. I am, however, quite convinced that the foundation for a new level of reincarnational experiences is established in part by the transmutation of the prior reincarnational trash. And when we transmute that low-level energy, we gain access to new insights and new information. We gain access to new tools like the Rays of Soul Integration, Rays Eight through Twelve. We can begin to anchor the Body of Light using the Tenth Ray into this physical dimension and thereby further establish the foundation for what is coming.

Our reincarnational trash weighs heavily on the planet herself. Earth is a living being. Just think if we all began to conceive of the Earth as a living organism. No really—what would that feel like? How would we see ourselves in relation to Earth? Our physical bodies support our consciousness. Earth supports both our physical and our mental bodies. How are we connected to Earth? Our cells support our lives and give us the ability to move through this third-dimensional reality. Are we not like our cells to Mother Earth? What service do we provide for the planet? What do we give back to Mother Earth? Do we just consume and deplete her energies, or do we amplify her energetic fields allowing for her growth?

As we consume the gifts that Earth provides for us—and when you think of it Mother Earth provides everything to support our physical existence—we leave the trash behind. And when we have our physical experiences and create all those lovely emotions related to them, we leave that behind also. Emotional pollution of the planet is just as real and most likely more toxic to her well-being than the physical pollution. When we focus on transmuting our lower-level emotions such as fear and anger, we detoxify the planet. As we work to unburden Earth from our toxic emotions, she is able to move to a higher energetic level and prepare along with us for the next chapter in reincarnational experiences.

Be the Change

My personal belief is that change happens all the time through the actions of individuals. It takes someone to begin the process, and then others start to join in. History is replete with the life stories of individuals. Think about the political movements of the twentieth century. Names like Lenin, Stalin, Hitler, Mussolini, Roosevelt, Churchill, and Mao come to mind. Think about the major religious movements throughout history, and you think of the Buddha, Moses, Jesus, Mohammad, Martin Luther, and more recently Mother Teresa and Martin Luther King, Jr. The list goes on and on. We see the contributions of individuals in science, art, and literature.

You have the opportunity to do your part in the New Awareness. It doesn't matter if they write books about your life or not. If you are ready to move forward with your experiences here in this third dimension, then begin the process of change. Ask yourself what is the next baby step you could take to move yourself forward?

Life is all about change. Some people struggle so hard against change. In reality, can you think of something that hasn't changed? Change is all around, even in your body. You are not the person you were yesterday. Millions of your cells have died and been replaced. Let's have a new mindset about change. Rather than fight it, let's embrace it and see how that works.

I mentioned at the beginning of this book that Julie and I received this information several years ago. I have shared this information through seminars, which I presented locally. My desire is to make this information available to as many people as possible. To that end, I have developed a video seminar that is available on the website. These videos are separated into short, easy to digest segments that focus on the key information presented in the book.

I am really excited about this next project, which I began working on while I was completing this book. I have teamed up with a gifted musician by the name of Richard Shulman, and together we have recorded music infused with the energy of the Rays. To the best of my knowledge, this has never been done before. For those of you who are more oriented to sound, this is a great way to musically connect with the energy of the Twelve Rays. The music is also available on the website, TheTwelveRays.com.

The Team has continued to work with us and there is more information that we will share in the future. But for now, focus on this very important work, your personal transformation, and live the life that you choose to live. Step into that awareness of who you truly are and create the life that leads to your happiness.

Be the creator that you are. Use the gifts that have been provided. They are a part of your heritage. You are God. Let your light shine, and as you do, all of creation rejoices.

Well done.

WORKS CITED

Alder, Vera Stanley. *The Finding of the Third Eye*. Boston: Weiser Books, 1970.

Bailey, Alice. *The Rays and the Initiations (A Treatise on the Seven Rays)*. New York: Lucis Publishing Company, 1993.

Byrne, Rhonda. *The Secret: The 10th Anniversary Edition*. New York: Atria Books, 2016.

Hill, Napoleon. *Think and Grow Rich*. Chatsworth: Wilshire Book Company, 1999.

Mulford, Prentice. *Thoughts Are Things*. North Charleston: Merchant Books, 2014.

Nightingale, Earl. *Earl Nightingale's Greatest Discovery: Six Words that Changed the Author's Life Can Ensure Success to Anyone Who Uses Them*. New York: Dodd Mead, 1987.

Proctor, Bob and Sandra Gallagher. *The Art of Living*. New York: Penguin Random House, 2013.

Proctor, Bob and Greg Reid. *Thoughts Are Things: Turning Your Ideas into Reality (Think and Grow Rich)*. New York: Tarcher Parigee, 2015.

United States Catholic Church. *A Catechism of Christian Doctrine, Prepared and Enjoined by Order of the Third Council of Baltimore (the Baltimore Catechism)*. Cincinnati: Mt. Washington Press, 2012.

THE AUTHOR'S STORY

I was born into a Catholic family in Buffalo, New York, in 1951, the third son in a family of four boys. The fourth son didn't live very long, and his death was traumatic for the entire family. I followed my older brothers through Catholic grade school, through the only Jesuit high school for boys in town, and I even attended the same Catholic college they graduated from. I received a very valuable gift from the Jesuits. They taught me how to think for myself.

While I was developing the ability to think critically, I realized that Catholic dogma was not working for me any longer. I didn't have a better answer to life's mysteries, so I decided to put the entire question of religion on the back burner. I hoped that somewhere along the road a reasonable alternative would show up.

I got married at the age of nineteen while attending college. Upon graduation, I took my small family to Germany and taught English in a German middle school for two years. Then I returned to Buffalo and attended graduate school. When I receive my graduate degree, I joined the blossoming computer industry as a computer programmer. I spent over twenty years in corporate America, got divorced, and never had time to revisit my religious beliefs until one day when a colleague of mine introduced me to New Age thought.

I left corporate America as an official "New Ager" and decided to do something meaningful with my life. I opened a wellness center that I named Phoenix Rising. It focused on alternative healing modalities and all sorts of New Age concepts. It was during this time that I met Julie. She introduced me to the Team. Needless to say, my life has never been the same.

My reality shifted. The answers that I had been looking for in my youth were beginning to unfold. The Team presented a source of information that we never had access to before. We never knew where a Team session was going to lead. And then one day they gave us the information about the Twelve Rays. They suggested that we write a book and share what we had been given.

It has taken over ten years to write this book, *The Reality of Your Greatness*. They gave us more information in addition to the Twelve Rays. We have more to share and we will. But in the meantime, Julie and I are sharing this information about the Rays through this book, through the music of the Twelve Rays, and through live workshops, video workshops, and webinars.

I am sharing with you my journey through the Twelve Rays, a journey that still continues to this day. My hope is that you find some of your life's answers within the pages of this book.

CHART OF THE RAYS

Rays of Aspect

Name	Color	Primary Function	Secondary Function
First Ray Divine Will	Red	Become the Creator of Self.	Identify resistance to change.
Second Ray Love and Wisdom	Luminescent aqua-blue	Connect with Divine Love.	Bring clarity to your thought.
Third Ray Active Intelligence	Golden Yellow	Identify what you need to do to manifest your goals.	Attract resources to you by focusing your attention.

Rays of Attributes

Name	Color	Primary Function	Secondary Function
Fourth Ray Harmony Through Conflict	Green	Resolve inner and outer conflict.	Help ground individuals who are too much in their head.
Fifth Ray Concrete Knowledge	Orange	Pursuit of knowledge	Help ground individuals who are too deeply involved with their emotions.
Sixth Ray Devotion and Idealism	Indigo Blue	Help individuals stay focused on personal goals.	Break old patterns and addictive behaviors.
Seventh Ray Gateway into Awareness	Violet	Dissolve the weightiness of past experience.	Raise individual energy levels.

Rays of Soul Integration

Name	Color	Primary Function	Secondary Function
Eighth Ray The Cleansing Ray	Violet and Green	Cleanse and balance those things that you no longer find necessary to hold.	Use it to bring clarity to your goals.
Ninth Ray Contact with the Soul Level	Luminescent Light Blue and Green	Loosen our association with our physical identities.	Establish contact with the soul-level part of self.
Tenth Ray The Body of Light	Luminescent Pearl Color, Pastel Blue and Pink Sparkles	Begin to anchor into this dimension this higher aspect of self.	Begin working with the Spiritual Microtron.
Eleventh Ray The Bridge to the New Awareness	Luminescent Orange-Pink	Remove the last remnants of past experience.	Create a bridge to the New Awareness.
Twelfth Ray The New Awareness	Luminescent Gold	Feeling connected to your whole self.	Consciously create as never before.

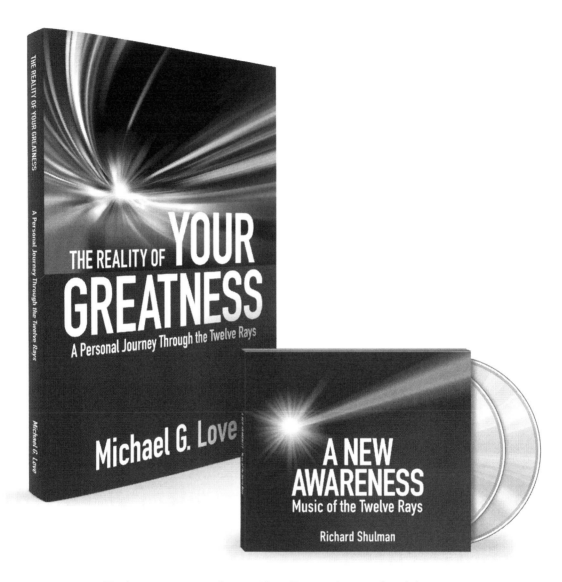

To learn more about the Rays through video seminars, webinars, and live workshops, visit **TheTwelveRays.com.** Sign up to receive advanced notice of upcoming events and special bonuses for members.